HOW A M....
BURNT MY BUM

HOW A MOZZIE BURNT MY BUM
And more comic shorts from

PETE PHEASANT

DB PUBLISHING

In memory of Alan Harries

First published 2022 by DB Publishing, an imprint of JMD Media Ltd,
Nottingham, United Kingdom.

Cartoons by Dave Hitchcock

ISBN 9781780916354

Printed in the UK

CONTENTS

MUSTN'T GRUMBLE?

GROWING UP

TOILET MATTERS

BEING DAD

LOSING THE PLOT

TV TIMES

SORT-OF POLITICS

DOMESTIC BLISS

WILDLIFE

TECHNOLOGY

FOOD

BLOKES AND CLOTHES

MANWATCHING

CHRISTMAS

BEING GRANDAD

WORDS

HOLIDAYS 168

GETTING OLD

THE END

MUSTN'T GRUMBLE?

Rise of the Whinger

IT is with alarming regularity that I look in the mirror of a morning and see TV grinch Victor Meldrew staring back. I've become an awkward customer.

There was a time when I'd stand quietly in shop queues while checkout girls discussed their love lives. In restaurants I'd simper 'fine, thanks' through mouthfuls of gristle au poivre when asked if everything was OK.

Concerning the question of man or mouse, I'd take the cheese every time.

Then something happened. I know not when or where, except that it coincided with fatherhood. I guess that standing up for my children – in parks, at parties and the like – gave me a new belligerence.

In just one week, I returned a pint of beer (dirty glass) and a packet of peanuts (warm from being stored near a lamp) at my local pub and fired off snotty letters about a new jacket (frayed lining), a pair of trousers (hole in pocket, resulting in change cascading down leg in chip shop) and a flat-pack wardrobe so riddled with faults that I wanted to run into the garden, find a branch and give it a Basil Fawlty-style thrashing.

My sons dreaded going with me to a certain high street cake shop in case I said 'thank you' in a loud and exaggerated manner because the staff had no manners. They cringed in memory of standing next to Dad in a bike shop while he held out for the Allen key missing from a flask holder he'd bought half an hour earlier.

The great thing about complaining is that it gets better with age. One day, I'll be able to wear my waistband under my nipples and chunter to myself in the street with impunity.

I'm thinking of forming a worldwide organisation, Whingers United. Think of the power we could wield.

The danger is that one can become cussed for the sake of it. Take my mate Des. He gleefully recalls the day he went supermarket shopping and decided to buy a pink grapefruit. There was no price tag, so he collared an assistant, who told him that the price was 25p and to ignore the sign in another aisle saying 40p.

As he picked up his cut-price fruit, Des should have felt a twinge of excitement. But he's such a deep-down misery-guts that he approached the till with foreboding.

And sure enough, the scanner said: pink grapefruit, 40p.

Des, of course, protested. He quoted the assistant word for word. A supervisor was summoned and made the mistake of asking if Sir could remember who'd given him such erroneous information.

It is at moments like these that the feeble cave in. Des, however, is made of sterner stuff. Not only could he remember, he could see the assistant a few yards away.

'Oi,' he called, 'come 'ere.'

Faced with the inevitable, the young man owned up. The supervisor's face resembled pink grapefruit as she mumbled an apology. In the circumstances, she said, the price was 25p.

Des was unimpressed. 'You can stuff it,' he said. 'I don't want it now.'

That's class.

The Great Fry-up Scandal

HOW mad can a grown man get about sausages? Just watch.

I know they're not good for my health. I don't care if they're made of pigs' nether regions.

I spend all week eating rabbit food in the hope that five portions of fruit and veg a day will balance out the many years of bad habits.

But come the weekend, I find food heaven occasionally in a good old fry-up.

It is, after all, a meal as British as fish and chips.

So, have you tried buying one on a Saturday afternoon?

I've done it often – try, that is. I recently visited a Derbyshire town that boasts two supermarket giants a few hundred yards apart. Both advertise a restaurant, so I headed for the least crowded. It was half past one in the afternoon – and the 'breakfast menu' had finished two hours earlier

Still, there was fish on offer. Shame it resembled the plastic variety that come in Christmas crackers and curl up on the palm of your hand to show how sexy you are.

There was also a vat of brown sludge with a crust on top marked 'chilli'.

Good job they were doing toasties. You can't go far wrong with a toastie.

'What toasties have you got, love?' I asked the woman at the till.

'Round t'corner,' came a surly voice from a vacant face. And sure enough, round t'corner was a tray containing packs of cheap white bread at £2.20 for cheese and ham. At least the cellophane wrapping looked appetising

Never mind, there was soup on the menu. That might go well with one of the brown, rock-like objects in a basket marked 'croutons'.

'No soup left,' said the man behind the counter.

No soup? It's a soup-ermarket, for chrissake! They'd got aisles full of the stuff a few yards away.

I should have complained – we all should – but I figured it would get me nowhere but high blood pressure.

Off to the car park I marched, convinced that a quick tour of the town centre would satisfy my yearning. Soon I was passing cafes aplenty. And, this being England, every single one was shut.

There was me thinking small businesses were struggling.

Big and small, they're seemingly united in an unholy anti-sausage dictatorship.

One well-known burger chain stops serving sausages and other 'breakfast' food at 10.30am. This means that at 10.29, little patties of pig meat are sizzling on a hot plate before being sandwiched in bread buns. At 10.31, they've been replaced by little patties of cow meat sizzling on the same sheet of metal.

Here's a radical idea: why not cook both and give me a choice? What hardship is it to them? I'd be much more likely to 'have a nice day' if I could order a sausage concoction at 10.29am and 61 seconds

Will someone explain the logic of this cut-off time for fry-ups? Is there a law against eating sausages in the afternoon?

Madness at the snack machine

SOMETHING very disturbing is taking place at the heart of everyday life and I can stay silent no longer.

It is the sort of insidious practice that erodes democracy and freedom of choice. I'm talking of the Great Snack Machine Scandal.

You might have seen the evidence at your workplace, school or leisure centre.

Let's say you want a Twix. And you can see a Twix. But you can't get at it because it's behind three Bounties.

Still, there's a KitKat, your second choice. But that's shielded by Snickers.

Mars can't get to you because there's a Galaxy in the way. Six tubes of Munchies stand proudly in line like Grenadier Guards but someone's put an Aero in front of them.

How on earth has this been allowed to happen?

I didn't see a public notice in the newspapers. Shouldn't there have been a planning application?

Don't tell me it's always been this way. That's what they want you to think; they chip away at your sanity until they can get any with anything.

I'm not so ga-ga that I don't recall a time when there was one row for one bar and one for another. Each in its place, as it should be. That's how it works with crisps. I mean, have you ever seen a bag of Mini Cheddars waiting behind salt 'n' vinegar? That would be ridiculous, right?

Yet we're expected to swallow this haphazard and downright unhealthy approach to chocolate – unhealthy, yes, because what we're in effect being told is that if we want a Twix, we have to eat three Bounties first. And I thought this government was worried about obesity.

As you might expect, I've tackled this at the highest level. The young man who fills our machine at work just happened to be there when I went in search of my favourite snack and found its way blocked, so I asked him straight, 'What is this madness?'

He looked at me as if I were the idiot and mumbled, 'It ain't my fault, mate. We've only got so many of each one on the van, like, and I just have to fill 'em up the best I can, yer know? I'm just doing what I'm told, mate.'

Call me a cantankerous old sod with nothing better to moan about but it's just not good enough.

Imagine going into a clothes shop to buy a shirt: you wouldn't expect to be denied a blue one because there were three whites in front of it, would you?

If I want a Twix and there's a vending machine containing such a snack, why can't I buy it when I want to?

Or am I expected to study my workmates' snacking habits and follow them to the vending machine at the very moment they're about to buy Bounty number three, just to make sure that no one gets at the last Twix before I do?

What do you think I am, some sort of weirdo?

Keeping up with the Boneses

THE most ridiculous and pointless tat-fest of the year is fast approaching. I'm talking Halloween.

Why on earth did we climb aboard this gravy train from America? Ah, I know: someone put a load of garish plastic in front of us and told us it would be a good idea to dress as ghouls, frighten old people into giving sweets to children and hand some of our hard-earned cash to filthy-rich businesses.

And so, for two weeks each year, we spend a fortune on dressing to spook and amuse. Plastic fangs, witches' hats, face paint and broomsticks are only part of the story as parents dress their little ones to keep up with the Boneses.

Halloween make-up, nails, wounds, ears, noses, masks, horns... shops and websites are awash with them. There's all manner of supposedly scary outfits on sale, including an 'Arab' and a 'sexy burka', predictably sparking howls of protest on social media (as if the rest of Halloween is in some way politically correct).

You can splash out on candles, spiders, cobwebs, glow sticks, chainsaws and even bloodstained stockings.

Why not carve a silly face in a pumpkin, then throw that potential source of nourishment in the bin?

And if you're thinking of having a quiet pint in your local anytime in the last few days of October (because, like Bonfire Night, it's no longer just a one-night affair), forget it because Halloween devotees will be partying like it's 1399.

Fancy a glass of snot, madam? That's a Halloween cocktail to you. How about a blood-red pudding full of eyes to see you through the week?

Perhaps you'd prefer something more delicate, like a rice paper picture of a flying witch stuck on too much cream on top of too little sponge in another vastly overrated American import, the cupcake.

If none of this appeals, you're as well off staying at home, hoping teenagers don't plaster your car with eggs as you draw the curtains and pretend you're not in so that you don't have to answer the door to a gaggle of little horrors playing trick or treat and watch the disappointment on their faces when you give them mini choc bars instead of a few quid.

Parents spend all year telling their children that nothing can hurt them but, come Halloween, they turn those same offspring into evil-looking creatures while at the same time assuring them that it's one big joke.

Here's an idea: don't make it up to knock it down; just don't do it.

Shut up and swim!

A VISIT to the local swimming pool is likely to reveal ladies of a certain age practising their unique sport.

It's called swarking. This mixture of swimming and talking requires very little stamina and a rudimentary swimming technique. Participants usually swark in pairs, though I have observed a threesome in action.

Essential qualities are a nice perm and the ability to chatter ceaselessly while remaining dry above the shoulders.

Swimming is Britain's most popular participation and top coaches say that going up and down at the same speed does little to improve fitness or help with slimming, Better, they say, to develop a strong stroke and push oneself in short bursts.

The swarker gives little for so-called experts. She believes that gentle circular movements of the hands, coupled with legs trailing idly in the water, will transform her from jelly bellied frump to finely honed beach goddess in the month before her holiday in Majorca.

During swarking, serious topics of conversation are frowned upon – metaphorically, of course, since any lapse in the rigidity of facial muscles might disturb the rhythm required to keep chin above water. Instead, conversations are peppered with phrases like 'I said to him' and 'have you seen the size of her lately?', preferably rehearsed in the car on the way to the baths.

Above all, the swarker understands the health benefits of swimming very slowly and ensuring that no one else in the pool disturbs her performance. If this means holding up an entire lane, so be it, for the swarker understands that good health is relative, so if others around her become more tense, she occupies a happier place.

And before anyone accuses me of sexism, be honest: have you ever seen doing men doing it?

Clearly, not everyone is a fan of the swarker. The middle-aged male torpedo, bent on going head-under hell for leather up and down the lanes until he's a red-faced soaking wreck who needs half an hour to recover in the changing rooms, has been known to protest that swarkers spoil his enjoyment.

One leisure centre responded by putting up 'please swim in single file only' signs. But the swarker is nothing if not resilient and pairs were soon spotted swimming in staggered file – the one in front on her back so that she could chat to her pal a few feet behind.

Perhaps we should ignore the grumps and capitalise on a national obsession by turning swarking into an Olympic sport. Marks could be awarded for irritation value, as judged by the faces of swimmers trying desperately to pass. Masking tape could be used in before-and-after tests to assess jaw strength.

I'm sure many a competitor would be waved off to the Games by her partner with best wishes and a muttered 'I always said you could talk for England'.

Phone pests

THE landline rings at home. It's about 10am. This can mean one of only two things.

I lift the receiver and say nothing, braced to slam it down at the sound of an automated message. But it's option two.

'Meester Feezant?' enquires an Asian voice.

'Pheasant,' I reply through gritted teeth.

'Good morning, Meester Feezant. I'm calling from the BT internet department.'

No you're not, you silly person, I'm thinking. You're probably in a basement in Mumbai, dozens of you in rows at desks with telephones and computer terminals, all trying to earn a crust by doing the dirty work for some Mr Big who pays you a pittance each time someone falls for one of his scams.

Besides, I don't have any dealings with BT and even if I did, they wouldn't phone me out of the blue with the sort of tale you're about to spin: that you've noticed that my internet connection is unsafe and that people have been hacking into my computer for illegal purposes but now you're here to help. And you're going to do that how exactly?

'Ah,' I say at last when the spiel is paused, 'so you want me to go to my computer so that you can show me where to find its IP address, and then I'm going to tell you what it is… and then you can hack into my computer and rob me blind?'

'No, Meester Feezant!'

'Do you think I've fallen off a Christmas tree? Now go away and take me off your database!'

And a fat lot of good that does me, because there are three or four similar calls during the next week – always at the same time. Mr Big must train them to know when wealthy westerners are at their dopiest.

Times must be hard in that Mumbai basement. The callers are mere minnows in a phishing expedition, doubtless run by the mafia in some form or other.

It probably needs just one success in thousands of attempts – one person daft enough to believe that someone is watching their computer's every move and has come to their rescue out of the goodness of their heart – for enough cash to be siphoned from bank accounts or enough debts run up on credit cards to pay the entire workforce for a week.

And the pittance the minnows take home might make the difference between food for the whole family or just the children.

Do I care? Not one jot. These people are crooks and the fact that they're poor crooks rather than wealthy ones makes no difference when they take my money. And here's the gigantic jigsaw in which they're tiny pieces: according to communications regulator Ofcom, UK consumers receive about 4.8 billion nuisance calls, 1.7 billion live sales calls, 1.5 billion silent calls, 940 million recorded sales messages and 200 million abandoned calls each year.

I've tried talking to the scam pests reasonably. I've tried the Telephone Preference Service. But they will not be told, so they will learn that the Pheasant might be a placid bird but, when cornered, it can turn nasty.

I won't use modern technology to fight this modern curse, just one of the oldest forms of alarm known to man. I intend to invest in a loud whistle with which to give nuisance callers' ears a bashing at the first sign of a lie.

This might hamper their earning potential somewhat by causing temporary deafness. And I realise it will have no effect on Mr Big, who will simply find someone else to fill their chair. But it will make me feel better.

A slice of cheek

THIS is the story of 4p and a sliced loaf.

Spurning the supermarkets for once, I called at a little bakery on the high street and asked for a 'small wholemeal', displayed on a shelf beside its price tag: 97p.

'Like that sliced, darling?' asked the shop assistant.

'Yes, please.'

She hurried into a back room and a machine whirred into action. Back she came with my loaf, sliced, and announced, 'That's one pound and a penny, please.'

For a tantalising moment I thought she might let me off the penny: save the business some useful change. But no. And having only a fiver on me, I left with four £1 coins and 99p of irritating shrapnel in my pocket.

It was only when I got outside that it hit me: I'd been overcharged and missed a chance to complain

OK, it was only 4p; mere crumbs in monetary terms. Not as if I couldn't afford it, and not an unreasonable, charge, perhaps, given that the bakery had had to buy, power and maintain the slicing machine.

But was this normal practice in bakeries? Had I gone through life not knowing about it? Surely, the correct approach would have been, 'Would you like that sliced, darling? That'll be 4p extra?' Then I'd have been happy.

My wife didn't seem unduly surprised when I told her later – not about the charge or about me making a big deal of it. She's had many years' practice at keeping a straight face over my ridiculous battles with the world.

But I was not about to let the matter drop. One does not become a grandmaster grinch by letting the bit slip from between one's teeth.

Next day, I decided to investigate. Driving to two supermarkets, I quickly ascertained that neither charged for slicing loves. Indeed, each had the same variety, one sliced, one unsliced, side by side at the same price.

By now I'd spent far more than 4p in time and petrol. But it's the principle that counts.

I phoned the shop later and politely told the manager what their standard practice should be vis a vis the slicing of loaves and charging thereof.

She agreed. In fact, she said, she would speak to the member of staff concerned, which left me thinking I'd better not risk buying anything from that assistant in future, in case she had to take it out of sight, whereupon she might do something ghastly to it.

Perhaps I'm being unreasonable. But this sort of thing can be the thin of the wedge, which is precisely what I'd set out to avoid by having a machine slice my bread.

GROWING UP

Scooter days and marble cricketers

LIKE many of my generation, I was driving a car before I rode a scooter. The vehicle was a huge Noddyesque creation, made of steel, powered by pedals and announced by a noisy horn.

Fifty-something years later, I have only hazy memories of my earliest days behind a wheel but I can vividly recall my only scooter. I was about 11 and wanted a Triang model, like some of my pals had. I loved the pneumatic-effect wheels and chrome spokes.

Christmas Eve arrived and, having long sent my wish list up the chimney to Santa, I prepared for an early night, hoping, as kids always do, that the sooner one sleeps, the sooner morning will come.

My parents put out a mince pie and a tot of rum – Dad, being an ex-Navy man, insisted this was Santa's favourite tipple – and packed me off to bed in a state of high excitement.

My grandparents had come to stay and Grandad had been given my bed, so I slept on the top of my brother's two-storey, iron-framed ex-hospital bunk, where the usual restful night was punctured by Grandad's pitiful sobs.

Every time he came to stay, the poor fellow cried his heart out through the night, so much so that I once woke him to ask what was wrong.

It took me years to understand he was snoring.

I'm sure I woke every half hour during every Christmas Eve of my childhood but I never once caught Santa in the act, though there was always a bulging pillowcase at the foot of the bed by 3am.

This year, something huge and half wrapped was propped against the wardrobe. I began to make out its shape and was at first disappointed. It was a scooter all right but a Mobo, not a Triang. Burnt orange in colour, it had the maker's name in yellow on the front column, and handle grips to match its solid black rubber tyres.

In the months to come, I learnt that the other man's grass is not always greener. All my mates loved my Mobo and it became both getaway vehicle and defender, speeding me to new adventures and away from neighbourhood bullies.

Big is not always best, however, and one of my most memorable Christmas gifts was one of the smallest and cheapest.

Marbles were popular in the 60s but 'Basil D'Oliveira' was something else.

Dad was a devil for surprises and, after Christmas Day tea – an elaborate affair of tinned red salmon and salad that no one really wanted – he'd pick up an ever-present Christmas decoration, a crude figure of Santa fashioned from cardboard tubes and red crepe paper, with a plastic face attached by elastic, and talk to it.

'A surprise you say, Santa. Well, let's see.'

And out of the cardboard belly he'd pull a little gift for each of us, evidently forgotten by Santa as he filled the pillowcases.

This year, mine was a bag of marbles. Now, marbles were common currency for kids who spent most of their time playing in the street, but I'd never seen any like these.

One fabulous translucent white specimen had a red and orange strip snaking around its circumference. This became Basil D'Oliveira, one of the great cricketers of my youth. Others I christened John Edrich, Tom Graveney and Fred Trueman and all went on to perform heroics in a game I invented and played all by myself on the best-room floor – marble cricket, with my left hand bowling a marble and my right guarding the matchbox of a wicket with an ice-lolly stick for a bat.

Unlike the scooter, this was not something I could talk about to my pals. But, for several years, there were few delights to equal a match-winning Test century peppered with fours to the piano stool boundary.

Rotten little me

SO much is said and written these days about anti-social behaviour that if you didn't know better, you'd think today's youngsters had invented it.

But, as my sons have been learning lately, I was no angel. In fact, I was a little horror at times.

We were spending a few days with their aunt and, since we lived a long way apart, our rare get-togethers invariably brought up tales of our childhood. As soon as my sister said, 'Can you remember when you wouldn't let me join your gang?' I could feel a cringe coming on.

The boys listened with glee as she told of her initiation test. Not only had I ordered her to take a running jump out of the bedroom of a derelict house on to an old mattress on the yard outside, I had insisted that her first attempt wasn't good enough because she'd run, stopped, then jumped, instead of taking a leap of faith.

She was nine years old at the time.

Nothing I say now can dim my shame. But that was the sort of price my kid sister and her twin brother, four years my junior, paid for hanging around with the big kids.

Besides, they were used to my nasty little ways. Only recently, my brother felt the need to remind me of my favourite instrument of torture when I was about 12.

Yackety, as I called him, consisted of a length of knicker elastic tied at one end around the hinges of a Rinstead Pastilles tin and at the other end around a heavy rubber doorstopper, about two inches thick.

With tin in hand, I was able to fire the doorstopper at arms and backsides with great effect, then whip the missile back to daddy.

Nevertheless, as gang members, my siblings were able to enjoy mischief beyond their years.

When we weren't door knocking or hedge hopping, we'd climb on to the roof of the town's public toilets and fire pea shooters at passersby.

Our favourite haunt was a long-abandoned former RAF camp. Its deserted and crumbling buildings were a playground paradise where we held stone throwing contests and raced along echoing corridors strewn with glass from the windows we'd smashed. We'd even jump through an old chute and land commando-style on the rough ground ten feet or so below.

I'd be horrified if my children played in such a place, but things were different then. There was less of a sense of danger when kids went out to play. Even before we were at secondary school, we'd wander miles from home to play in secluded woods and fields, where anything might have happened to us, and our parents had no idea where we were from breakfast to teatime.

Another top location was a neglected farm, where we'd picnic among the cowpats and clamber along a huge fallen-down tree, the same tree on which my best friend was sitting when he failed to hear me shout that I'd fired my new bow at a branch, and the metal-tipped arrow sank into his shin.

But, for all the hazards, there were very few accidents and it's sad that today's children can't enjoy similar freedom. Having read my confession, however, you might think that endless hours playing video games might produce more rounded human beings.

Mystery of the green nipple

MY first school reunion in 30 years was, as expected, a strange affair. It was also momentous for two reasons I could not have foretold.

I'd approached the get-together with some trepidation. After all, most of us had had no contact since leaving school in 1970. But, after a few minutes in the pub where we'd done much of our underage drinking, I felt I was in the company of friends.

I was met by a sea of smiling, vaguely familiar faces and a chorus of 'Sid!' (my secondary school nickname, for reasons too daft to mention) and before long we were finding out what had happened in the intervening years and giggling drunkenly at memories of the old days.

Finding myself immersed in the bonhomie of virtual strangers, I thought we'd aged pretty well, though whether the rest thought the same about me is another matter. Then I heard some stunning news: one of our old teachers had recently retired. Stunning because I thought he'd looked past it 30 years earlier.

Everybody over 20 looked old in the 1960s. I used to help out in my dad's barber shop, selling combs and Brylcreem to people who knocked on the frosted-glass window of the off-sales. Every so often, someone in a trilby and raincoat would ask to see Dad and he'd reach under a counter and slide them 'something for the weekend'.

I knew what they were, of course: I'd pinched a packet and blown them up in the crowd at a football match. What I couldn't understand was what those old fogeys wanted with them. Little did I realise that they were the studs of their generation.

My generation, though, were much cooler, weren't we?

Or did our kids look at us in much the same way?

With tongues ever looser as the reunion party wore on, I reminded an old classmate of an intimate detail concerning his former girlfriend. I knew of this not from personal experience but, as I recalled, because he'd told me. Or someone else had. Anyway, it was a known fact: the poor girl had an unusual, erm, well, one of her, er...

She had one green nipple, which sounds like the first line of a song.

Or so the story went.

The ex-boyfriend creased up laughing. He'd never heard the story, he said, and it most certainly wasn't true.

So disconcerting was this discovery that, in the beer haze of the morning after, I began to wonder what other schoolboy 'facts' in my mental baggage were without foundation.

Was Mao Tse Tung's Little Red Book actually yellow? Was JFK's assassination a hoax?

And was there ever a more boring subject than the history of medieval strip farming?

Chuffing for England

ANOTHER national No Smoking Day has been and gone and I'm afraid I'm still in the grip of the evil weed.

I've been a smoker for the best part of 40 years, on and off, but can honestly say that I'm now down to the odd one or two, when I go out for the evening. I can't promise that I'll ever stop for good but I know I'll never again be a 30- or 40-a-day man.

Looking back to my 20s, I wonder how I found the time to do anything else but smoke, and the cost doesn't bear thinking about. Such is the power of Old Nic that, no matter how much I saved when I stopped, I'd always find the money when I started again.

I like to think I've taught my children a few good lessons but when it comes to smoking, I've let them down. Thankfully, both detest the habit and I'd bet their inheritance that they'll never succumb.

Of course, they've grown up in a very different world to that of my youth.

It doesn't seem long since I was working in an office where eight of the ten staff smoked – at their desks and sometimes when dealing face to face with customers.

Back in the 1950s and '60s, smoking was portrayed as a manly, sophisticated thing to do and as soon as I'd salted away enough pocket money, I bought a pack of ten Regent for 1s 10d (about 9p today). I told the shopkeeper they were for my mum but smoked them on my paper round over the next week or so. I was just 11.

Far from carrying a government health warning, cigarettes were endorsed by contemporary role models, with the face of a handsome Royal Navy sailor adorning many packs.

Both my parents smoked heavily and no Christmas gift made my father's eyes light up more than a 50 pack of Park Drive.

My maternal grandparents smoked what I regarded as posh brands – Player's Plain and Senior Service – and both had the knack of making a cigarette last half an hour, with two inches of ash balanced precariously on a nub-end.

I can still picture Grandad in the changing rooms of our local swimming baths, lodging a half smoked Wills Whiff on the cubicle wall as he stripped to his trunks and prepared to give his lungs some healthier exercise.

Stranger still was the example set by sporting heroes of the day.

I vividly remember attending my first Test match, as a 1960s schoolboy. England were playing India at Trent Bridge and I was thrilled to have a seat near the boundary.

Freddie Trueman, the legendary fast bowler, was fielding only a few yards away… and I was not at all surprised to see a cigarette smouldering between his fingers.

TOILET MATTERS

Dept. of Bogs and Brushes

THERE was a sharp intake of breath from the man from DOBS (Department of Bogs and Sinks) when I got through on his direct line. Then I explained that I'd found the number scrawled on a toilet door.

'I see, sir,' he said. 'So how can I help?'

'Well,' I said, 'I've just had an awful time shopping. I was at the big retail park in Anytown when I just had to go.'

'Go, sir? Where?'

'You know – for a wee.'

'Ah, not very well prepared, weren't we, sir?'

'It's not that simple when you get to my age,' I said. 'The bladder's not as patient as it used to be. Anyway, I was in Currys, buying a new cooker, when I came over fit to burst. They didn't have a toilet for customers but said there was one at the shop next door.'

'Did they indeed?'

'So, I ran there as fast as my crossed legs could carry me but their loo was out of order and there wasn't another on the whole estate. Can you believe that? There must be 20 stores there, with hundreds – probably thousands – of shoppers at any one time, yet there's not one public toilet. It's scandalous.'

'Now, now, sir, let's not exaggerate.'

'That's easy for you to say. I thought I was going to have to slip behind a building and…'

'Careful, sir. We don't want to incriminate ourselves, do we?'

'Don't worry, I didn't fancy the fine. But I did something worse. I got into my car and drove to McDonald's. They've got a loo, thank goodness, so I sneaked in. Mind you, the staff chased me across the car park afterwards, shouting "have a nice day".'

'So,' said the man from DOBS, 'all's well that ends well.'

'Not quite. When I got home, I decided I couldn't let the matter rest, so I looked on the internet and…'

'Ah, the internet. Such a danger in the wrong hands, sir.'

'Quite. But I wanted to know if there were any laws on the provision of public toilets in shopping areas.'

'And?'

'Apparently, there's no actual legislation but there is a British Standard that makes certain recommendations.'

'Really, sir?'

'Yes, really. And frankly I was appalled by what I found. It seems there are recommended standards for women but not for men.'

'I couldn't possibly confirm or deny that,' said the man from DOBS.

'Why on earth not?' I spluttered. 'It's not a state secret, is it?'

'Come, come, sir – we don't have secrets in this country.'

'Oh, this is ridiculous! Look, the report I found said the latest position is covered by British Standard 6465.'

There was a gasp. 'Oh dear,' he said at last.

'So I thought if I could find out what BS 6465 says, I'd know my rights.'

'Ah yes, rights,' said the man from DOBS. 'Everyone talks of rights these days. But what about responsibilities, sir?'

'Precisely! What about the responsibilities of shopkeepers who drain millions out of people like me but won't spend a few pee – pardon the pun – on giving us a glorified drain here and there?'

'You're not a communist, are you, sir?'

'Communist, no; columnist yes. Anyway, I eventually found BS 6465 on the internet. Or rather, a description of it. Seems you can't simply read it – you have to buy it. And it costs a hundred quid.'

'Naturally, sir.'

'What's natural about that? My taxes help to pay for the British Standards Institute.'

'With respect, sir, the country would go down the pan if organisations simply gave information away. Now, tell me how I can help.'

'Well, you must have a copy of BS 6465, so could you read the right bit to me?'

'Oh, I couldn't possibly do that, sir.'

'Why?'

'You've got the wrong department, sir. This is Bogs and Brushes: Standards of Cleanliness thereof. You need CURD.'

'What on earth's CURD?'

'Cubicles and Urinals in Retail Developments, sir. Formerly POTS – Provision of Toilets in Shops. We civil servants like a good acronym.'

'Sounds to me like you're taking the…'

'Policy of government seriously? Yes, sir. Goodbye.'

Cream gets a bum deal

THANKS to one of the great inventions of our times, recordable TV, I can not only watch what I want when I want but can fast-forward through the blather and skip the commercials.

On one occasion recently, though, my button thumb must have nodded off because I found myself watching, with incredulity, an ad for haemorrhoids cream.

Trouble in the nether regions is not easy to talk about, let alone endure, and I can only admire the advertising agency that rebranded Anusol by using images of fruit and other items that look a bit like bottoms to address the sensitive subject of piles, also known as 'the grapes of wrath' and 'Johnny Giles', after a former Leeds United footballer, who can't possibly have foreseen such a legacy when he entered the professional game.

My sympathy ends, however, with the bizarre pronunciation employed in the new ad, 'An-you-sol'.

What, I spluttered, were they talking about? Were they trying to hide the fact that this was something for the anus?

I'm not especially familiar with the product, but enough to know it had always been pronounced 'Ay-nuss-ol', leaving no doubt as to what part of the body it was intended for.

I could have seen some logic in the commercial if the first two syllables meant anything on their own but I've never heard of an 'an-you'.

Personally, I'd have gone for a name with connotations of a space-age zapper, like Endroids.

Come to think of it, though, 'sol' is halfway to the French for 'sun', so perhaps the marketing folk hoped to convey the impression of a fresh beginning, 'a new sun' – where it most certainly don't shine.

* * *

TALKING of bums, I've received another wonderful invention: the do-it-yourself bowel cancer screening kit.

This envelope of delights comes through the post every two years to those of us aged 60-plus and helps clinicians to decide if we need tests to show whether we have bowel cancer.

The NHS says 2,500 lives could be saved each year as a result of screening. Definitely not to be sniffed at.

For those of more tender years, I will refrain from detailing the mechanics of home testing, since it involves something resembling an ice-lolly stick and much ungainly posturing in the bathroom. But if ever someone comes up with a YouTube channel especially for geriatrics, the footage would make for hysterical viewing.

Meanwhile, I raise a glass to our wonderful NHS. Bottoms up!

Flatulence gets you nowhere

THESE are dark days. The wind of change is blowing through northern Africa and, in another corner of that vast continent, the wind of human bodies is threatening a global crisis.

It seems that Malawi's leaders have clashed over a new law which could make it an offence for anyone to break wind in public.

The row involves the country's Local Courts Bill, which, according to justice minister George Chaponda, would criminalise flatulence in a move designed to promote public decency.

The bill says, 'Any person who vitiates the atmosphere in any place so as to make it noxious to the public to the health of persons in general dwelling or carrying on business in the neighbourhood or passing along a public way shall be guilty of a misdemeanour.'

The country's solicitor general, Anthony Kamanga, says Mr Chaponda is talking out of his, um, out of the back of his head. He insists the controversial clause applies to pollution.

But western diplomats are alarmed. They believe the issue could have even serious repercussions for flatulence-friendly democracies than recent political unrest in Egypt and Algeria.

Flatulence fundamentalists are said to be bent on creating a wind-free state in the Middle East.

One influential figure, Mustapha Parp, has called for babies to be surgically fitted at birth with tell-tale balloons and a special police force to be set up to detect wrong do-do-ers.

'From the age of five, any child whose trousers showed signs of an inflated balloon would be dealt with severely,' Parp said, according to the respected French journal *Le Pétomane*.

Western observers fear that if Malawi falls to the odourless-trouser lobby, pressure for similar restrictions around the globe could be irresistible

Curry houses are watching nervously. In America, billionaire businessman Donald Trump has gone into hiding.

Mere words associated with what many regard as a natural, if somewhat anti-social, habit could be outlawed if the zealots have their way. The creators of TV cartoon series *The Simpsons* are said to have doctored Bart's famous song about baked beans so that it reads:

Beans, beans, the musical fruit.
The more you eat,
The more you have a fizzy tummy

Nowhere would a ban be more controversial than here in Britain, whose liberal attitude was epitomised in the popular TV series *Blackadder* by Baron von Richthoven, incredulous at 'you English and your amusing jokes about ze breaking of ze vind!'

The UK government is weighing the risk of mass civil disobedience against the benefits of a windfall tax on law breakers.

A leaked report by Sir Jasper 'the rasper' Boggins, special adviser to the cabinet, says that adopting the Malawi approach would rob the British entertainment industry of a rich source of material. The report adds, 'The right to break wind from an early age as a free and amusing pastime is enshrined in British life. Even in the royal household, children studying Latin recite *Qua sententia exsisto, permissum thy ventus vado solvo* (Wherever thou be, let thy wind go free).'

On the streets of Nottingham last night, news of a possible wind-breaking witch hunt was greeted stoically. As one man told this reporter, 'They can legislate all they like but they'll never find the guilty party in a crowded lift.'

No shame in a lady wee

WARNING: the following is intended as a serious discourse on changing habits and is not to be construed as puerile toilet talk.

So, a few questions for the chaps, though female readers might be interested in the answers.

Do you find yourself occasionally doing a lady wee?

If so, do you feel slightly ashamed, as if your masculinity might be called into question if you were to come out of the, um, water closet?

Or do you simply find sitting down to take a leak more practical and comfortable than the traditional approach?

I only ask because I've found myself doing it more recently. And discreet inquiries among friends and family suggest I am far from alone.

Let's skip the bodily details, suffice to say the practice suits me better, at certain times, in the right place.

I wouldn't risk it in public urinals (a place where, I should perhaps explain for the benefit of lady readers, men fall largely into two categories: the peepers and the peeped at).

But in the privacy of my own home, or somewhere else I know to be clean, or where the seat won't stay back, why not?

Anyway, who decided that men were supposed to do it standing up? It was the only option once upon a time. Then civilisation gave us the sit-down loo – yet men were expected to join a lavatorial rifle range, with the target several feet away. A case of stand, aim, fire… and don't leave it for the wife to clean up.

When I raised this subject with a few male friends and relatives, some appeared astonished or affronted by the suggestion but a small minority admitted sheepishly that they, too, fell into girlie ways now and again and knew others who did. Their ages ranged from the medically challenged mid-60s to healthy 20-somethings.

Was it ever thus, but never talked about? Somehow, I can't imagine it was pub talk among the miners and steelworkers of my grandparents' generation.

Perhaps it's another sign of the barriers between the sexes coming down in this enlightened age. It's 50 years since a Kinks song told us 'girls will be boys and boys will be girls, it's a mixed-up, muddled-up, shook-up world' and look at us now. Men no longer feel under so much pressure to be 'macho' and the world's a better place for that, though I fear that if the puritanical lobby that demonises wolf-whistling builders, Page 3 girls and the slightest hint of a sexist remark gets too carried away, we might forget what makes us want to make babies.

I hope my personal revelation puts some men at ease.

But the need to add a health and safety warning struck me one night after my bladder's regular mid-sleep alarm went off. With only the landing light to guide me, I walked the familiar route to the bathroom, enjoyed a little seated relief in the dark, washed and dried my hands, turned to leave – and walked straight into the edge of the bathroom door, narrowly missing my nose but causing a sickening crack on the forehead.

I think that's what's known as a lightbulb moment.

BEING DAD

Like father, like son

COME ON, own up: who's spent the days since schools broke up copying their little one's first, wonderful report and dispatching it around the globe to proud relatives?

My sons are long past that stage, the one where you blink back tears at Open Evening as Teacher says they're such well-mannered boys, etc, etc – or suppress a giggle as Teacher explains that dropping one's trousers in class is 'inappropriate behaviour'.

Mine are both at secondary school now and though this year's reports and Open Evenings brought much to make mum and dad proud, phrases like 'needs to avoid being distracted by other pupils' were a common thread… just as they were in my reports.

Teachers, it seems, are resigned to boys being boys. They just can't help messing about – and doing well in lessons in simply 'not cool'.

Spot the difference – my school report at 13.

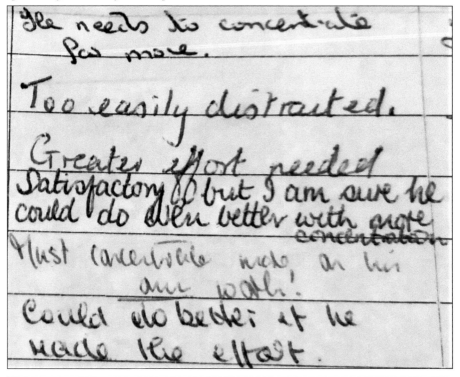

I was telling a teacher friend about my sons' reports. He simply smiled and said, 'They're lads, aren't they?' I blame the testosterone. They may be only 12 and 15 but my pair could get an A-level in double entendres, brow-furrowing, contemptuous snorting and full-on flouncing.

Once upon a time the only wildlife they craved was featured in nature documentaries. Now, the telly is dominated by American teen soaps full of bad jokes, weak acting and… ah, yes, pretty girls in tight trousers.

I'll sure they'll managed to overcome the distractions long enough to do well at school. They just need to concentrate a bit more and stop the silliness – though my lectures on this score took a battering recently.

We'd come across one of my old school exercise books. I was 14 and entering my thoughtful period, The lads had read my essays on junkies, racial harmony and other weighty topics. I think they were impressed. Then they came across a poem that began:

I am Sid the slug
I have an ugly mug
My dad who is a cat
Likes eating boiled fat.

Beside it the teacher had written in red pen: '3/10. Silly'
But enough of me. Do as I say, not as I do, eh?

Teenager gave me driving lesson

MY sons returned from school the other day to find this note pinned to the PC, 'To whom it may concern, I hereby give notice that from 8pm until 9.30pm tonight, this computer will be used by me.

'Furthermore, I wish to announce that I am having the coming weekend off duty – ie, I will not be giving any lifts to football or cricket practice unless those who wish to avail themselves of this service make efforts towards tidying up this house, washing/drying pots, etc.'

If nothing else it caused a chuckle or two.

The lads are 14 and 16 and simply the greatest. But keeping the house tidy is not one of their strong points and in a few years' time, I'll probably be found, perfectly preserved, waving a tea towel and mouthing 'please' beneath a mountain of chocolate wrappers, dirty socks, Coke tins and other assorted crud.

In the testosterone-charged air of Chez Phez, I'm fast becoming a joke, so I've decided I might as well laugh along. I say this without bitterness: we're still mates and love each other dearly but they're no longer Bambis following Dad's enormous antlers; a more a case of stags at bay.

It seems that the older and more mature they get, the older and more childish I become.

Once upon a time, a hammer blow to the knuckles during a spot of DIY might have provoked a mild oath. These days, the sounds of stamping feet and screamed obscenities can be heard out in the street.

But times are a-changing. On taxi duty at the weekend, I announced that I'd given up abusing fellow drivers who misbehaved.

No more hand signals of the type not found in the Highway Code, I vowed. Instead, I'd blow a kiss or give a cheery wave to speed the sad souls along life's highway.

Temptation came almost immediately. Nearing a busy island, I was hooted at by someone who presumably felt (wrongly) that I'd cut him up.

Down came my window, out went the hand, up went a friendly wave.

But soon he was weaving dangerously in front of me, causing me to brake sharply and hoot furiously – at which he let down his window and gave a little wave back.

Thankfully, the calming presence of my 16-year-old passenger made me abandon thoughts of an angry chase, and I followed the moron at a safe distance until he turned off.

Then he stopped to shoot me a glare.

And there I lost it. The wave formed in my mind but the two-fingered salute had a mind of its own.

See what happens when you try to be nice?

How green is my pizza?

I WAS showered, shaved, fed and ready for work before the rest of the family were up, so I left the kids a Post-it Note.

Mine may not be a family of note but we're certainly a family of notes – 'boys, have a nice day, love Dad'; 'Mum, gone to pictures, back late', that sort of thing.

What began as a bit of fun is now a vital tool of communication in a busy household, as we all go in different directions for most of the time.

On this particular day there was a serious point. The note contained an anagram, LICE SUM TON, with a request to the boys to call me when they'd cracked it, then claim their prize. It meant MELON IS CUT. I'd left it in the fridge, de-seeded, sliced and covered to await hungry mouths. The prize, of course, was a slice of melon.

The boys might be 16 and 19 but I still worry about their diet. Red meat and eggs were good for you when I was young. Now, we're told, it's fruit and veg, so I go to great lengths to get them to eat five portions a day – but do you know how much that is?

I looked it up on the internet and was amazed. For a family of four, five portions of fruit or veg a day for a week constitutes, for example, 28 bananas, 28 dessert bowls full of salad, 84 heaped tablespoons of peas, five litres of orange juice and 728 grapes. The experts count a cupful of grapes as a portion. I managed to get 26 grapes in a cup, but it's not much of a drink.

To my sons' dismay, toast and jam does not count.

Buying that little lot, or its equivalent, is one thing. Getting them to eat it is quite another. Whole apples seem to present an unbearable challenge to their weary teenaged bodies. The thought of opening the fridge and plucking grapes from a bunch makes them want to lie down. But sneak a pack of apple slice into their lunchboxes or waft a bowl of washed grapes under their noses and we're two portions down and three to go.

I stumbled across another method quite by accident during a day off work. I'd prepared a healthy salad – oh, and pepperoni pizza – for me and the youngest son. It was ready to eat the moment he walked in from school and he was delighted that, for once, Dad hadn't spent the afternoon whipping up some cunning recipe to disguise a portion of healthy fish.

We each ate a quarter of the pizza, leaving the rest in the oven on a tray that Mum had forgotten to put away. It was when he bit into his second slice that he spluttered, 'Urgh! This tastes of soap!'

And he was right – but I couldn't understand why until I examined the baking tray. Mum hadn't simply left it out, she'd drizzled it with Fairy Liquid and left the detergent to cut through the grease from a previous meal.

Still, I managed to get something green down the boy that day.

Where have all the nicknames gone?

I'VE noticed something very old-fashioned about the rebellious, hoodie-wearing schoolboys of today.

They call their best friends by their surnames – not clipped or extended to sound cooler, just plain Smith or Jones. The gangsta generation has gone all public school.

A nickname was obligatory when I was at school and if you had any sense, you'd invent your own before your friends came up with something nasty. I've not seen most of my classmates for 30-odd years but they'll always be Lol, Ces, Cob, Pot, Dobber and Chang, to name a few.

Both my sons are exceptions to the current trend. They have, and always will be, known as Phez, just as I am.

I often get giggling girls knocking at the door and asking, 'Is Phez in?' To which I delight in replying, 'You're looking at him. Did you want Son of Phez?'

*   *   *

HAVE you ever been cupcaked? Forget those spongy, chocolate-topped goodies that were once a teatime treat. I'm talking of a craze that's doing the rounds among my youngest son and his mates.

It consists of breaking wind into cupped palms and pushing them under someone's nose. I suspect they earn extra credits for cupcaking a parent.

It's oddly reassuring to know that kids are as fond of toilet humour as ever they were.

My baby's leaving home

I'M sorry. I know you've come to expect frippery in this column but today I need a shoulder to cry on. My little boy's leaving home.

OK, so he's 19 and big enough to toss me around like a rag doll if I didn't know his ticklish spots so well. But he's still my baby and ever since he announced that he planned to move into a house with three mates, I've spent a lot of time gulping and telling myself to be a brave daddy.

'Pull yourself together, man!' you might say. 'It'll do him the world of good/make a man of him/show him what life's really about.'

And you'd be right. After all, he's only going for six months, he says. Then he'll be back, he says. He wants a taste of independence, and that's perfectly natural, isn't it? I mean, it's not as if I didn't know this day would come eventually.

He has a car, so he doesn't need Dad's Taxi. He has a steady girlfriend, so he no longer relies entirely on the family for love. He's working and doesn't need Dad's Bank for survival.

It's just that I didn't expect it, not yet. I thought I'd have time to prepare for the moment, which is silly, because I've learnt that grand plans don't stand a chance against the toss of life's dice.

Dan, on the other hand, is young and full of hope. He's discovered the outside world and there's no turning back. Vast new horizons beckon and he relishes each step with a sense of adventure and excitement that I vaguely remember.

I've tried to put him off, telling him to stay at home and save his money instead of putting it into a landlord's pocket.

But the power I could once wield over him (helped by cajoling, threats and downright blackmail) has left me, and besides, it's only when you've left home that you realise how well off you were when 'board' was your biggest outgoing.

I can't help feeling, though, that I've failed in some way because he no longer wants to share my home.

It's illogical, I know, and I'd better get used to the inevitable. So, I'll try to be positive. When he sets off with his suitcase, he'll go with bags of love, support and encouragement.

I'll tell him to have fun and take care until he's back in next to no time, during which we (well, his mum) will keep his bedroom in a rare state of tidiness.

Then I'll go inside, reach for the hankies and wonder: Do we ever let go?

Oh no, he isn't!

THE ink had barely dried on my last column when I was reminded once more that kids never tire of making a mug of their parents.

A day after I'd written about his departure, eldest son Dan phoned to say he wasn't moving out after all. The deal he'd planned with a few friends over a house in the big, bad city had fallen through.

'But I've just written about you,' I protested.

'Ah well,' he chirped, 'you can write a follow-up.'

That's my boy: 19 years of living with a journalist had taught him well.

I'm relieved, naturally, and thrilled that he's going to be getting in my way for a little longer, even though our various work and social commitments mean we see each other fleetingly for the most part, and then I can't help nagging him to stop shovelling his food/licking his knife/leaving his gigantic shoes all over the place for me to fall over.

I've also been doing some reflection and have come to the conclusion that it wasn't independence and the bright city lights that lured him away after all.

It seems I was to blame, because when we'd first talked, hypothetically, about him leaving home and he'd said he wanted to get some money behind him first and would probably be with us until he was 30, I'd snorted, 'You needn't bother. I want the chance to come home from work and ravish your mum in the middle of the day, before we get too old.'

'Urgh!' he'd said. 'Pass me the sick bag,'

Bigger, hairier and daft as ever

MOCKED at home, at work and on the telly: there's no hope for me.

B&Q have a cheek. How on earth did they get me into their new TV ad about DIY disasters? The face and bodies of the incompetents taking part might be different but there's no mistaking the lack of dexterity and spatial awareness required to turn simple tasks into chaos.

I'll be seeing my lawyers.

Worse still, someone's been filming in my house without permission. This is the only explanation for the Channel 4 sitcom *Friday Night Dinner*, a brilliant portrayal of what happens when grown-up kids return to Mum and Dad's once a week.

Ours come home on Sunday and I can vouch for the sitcom's painful realism: the naïve put-upon mum; the dad who makes inappropriate sexual remarks and mangles his swear words; the 'boys' still trying to out-prank each other in their 20s.

We saw the show for the first time when our own daft, lolloping pair – hairier, larger and gruffer than their five-year-old alter egos but otherwise identical – joined us for a Sunday roast, after which they stuck their fingers in the chocolate trifle and poked them in each other's ears.

Naturally, as I tried to restore order, I got one, too, so I responded in the way mature dads do: I filled a plastic bottle with water and let the eldest, Dan, have it full in the midriff.

The humiliations that come with being older, frailer and balder than my offspring might be easier to endure if I knew that when I went to work, my PC would function properly. So, on the third consecutive morning of being unable to see my emails, I was not happy as I phoned the IT desk.

I was so tetchy, in fact, that the IT expert gave up trying to talk me through the start-up process that he logged on to do it himself. As I witnessed the ever-spooky spectacle of a cursor moving about my screen with no help from me, a text message arrived from Dan: his firm had just called everyone into a meeting and announced 200 redundancies. He had three months to find a new job.

It couldn't have come at a worse time, with his wedding on the way and a large bill from the vet pay.

I felt as all parents do at such times: as sick with hurt for my little one as if he'd fallen down and grazed a knee.

'Oh no!' I texted back, oblivious of the date. 'So sorry.'

Then I did what any journalist in a busy newsroom would do: I scribbled a note about the job cuts and handed it to my editor, who was conducting the morning editorial conference a few desks away.

Minutes later, another text arrived, 'Ha ha, April fool!'

'You rotten little…' I replied.

He must have sensed that I was not amused because he promptly phoned to ask, between giggles, if he could – I don't quite know how to say this without choking – *buy me lunch* to make amends.

Meanwhile, brother Joe had texted him to say he'd spotted Dan's fiancée with another man. Then he'd sent mum a message to say his car had been vandalised. And Dan had called home, posing as someone from the Department of Work and Pensions and had managed to fool his mother for several minutes.

Boys, eh? Do we ever grow up?

LOSING THE PLOT

Specs in the bread bin

I'M working towards a degree in scattiness and expect to graduate with first-class honours.

Barely a day goes by without an exemplary piece of fieldwork.

My spectacles are a major source of confusion and amusement, forever escaping their case and hiding in odd places, like the bread bin or on top of a wardrobe.

Mobile phones are another. My wife aimed a few rude words in my direction one night when, having made the customary checks on doors and plugs in readiness for bed, I prowled the living room, mouthing to her 'where's my phone?' – while holding it to one ear as I listened to a voicemail.

On another occasion I tried to operate the works car park barrier with the card I keep in my phone case, only to find I'd picked up my wife's phone by mistake. So, I called my phone on hers to let her know… and was surprised to hear my phone ringing in my jacket on the back seat of the car.

This scholarly pursuit of the ridiculous can have its dangers, like the time I waved goodbye to my grandchildren while entering the revolving door of the reception area where I work. As I turned again and again to catch a glimpse of their smiling faces, I forgot about following the door on its natural course and walked, with a thud, into its glass surrounds.

My petrol station antics will take some beating, though. I'd not long owned my present car when I called there, reached for the pump and realised that the petrol cap was on the other side. So flustered was I that instead of getting back behind the wheel to turn the car around, I found myself opening a back door and climbing into the seat behind the driver's, where I promptly tried to make out it was intentional by rummaging around on the floor.

I have visions of stepping on to a stage to receive my degree from the University of Scattiness while wearing a half-open dressing gown and a Wee Willie Winkie-style nightcap.

Perhaps I should take this more seriously, see a doctor, ask about possible early onset dementia – or keep laughing at myself and sharing my little escapades with those similarly aged and bewildered, to reassure them that they are not alone.

Screwball gardening

LIFE is full of old sayings the older one gets and 'he's got a screw loose' seemed particularly apt as I tackled a project in the garden.

Now, you're more likely to hear me say 'I like going to the dentist' than 'I enjoy gardening'. For several decades, I'd left what vaguely resembles a lawn to the wiles of rampant weeds. I once had to borrow a scythe to cut a path through waist-high nettles just so that my wife could hang the washing out.

And they say that romance is dead.

But I am at last making an effort. Nothing to trouble Alan Titchmarsh, you understand; just a few borders, built from sections of wooden pallets, that I've filled with bark chippings. They will at least give the place a semblance of order and afford me a break from the battle against docks and dandelions.

All was going well until a piece of timber split under the rain of lump-hammer blows. Nothing that couldn't be fixed without a couple of screws, though, and I had just the thing: a handy carry-case containing hundreds of them, sorted by size into eight compartments. It was a gift from my sister, who had witnessed my DIY exploits with much amusement over the years and thought it would save me from curse-laden rummaging in a Tupperware pot where screws of all shapes and sizes mingled in finger-piercing anticipation.

I reached for my case of screwdrivers – another gift – and found one just right for the screws I'd chosen. The repair was soon effected and I ploughed on, with some success. My labours done for the day, I began to pack the tools away, picking up the case of screwdrivers with one hand and the case of screws with the other.

But I'd forgotten to fasten the screw case – and its entire contents spilt on to the lawn.

There followed the sight of an old man on his knees, face almost touching the grass as the sun bore down on his bald pate and his fingers sought out what remained of the set of 1,200 screws – most of them! – mindful that if he left one behind, it might one day connect with a lawnmower blade and he'd end up at A&E with a screw in his forehead.

How a mozzie burnt my bum

I'M wrestling with a condition called WWF. It has nothing to do with Hulk Hogan types throwing themselves around in mock combat but it does pit me against a superior foe.

WWF stands for Why Whitepaint on Finger, a tell-tale sign that has ladies of a certain age cooing in admiration. It denotes that the bearer has been decorating – a pursuit I hate with a passion almost as fierce as my loathing of cucumber.

I am constantly amazed that man can invent flying machines but can't devise a home decorating kit that works by itself.

It can't be too difficult to create a paint bomb that one places in the middle of the room and activates with a simple fuse, then makes a run for it, returning a few hours later to find walls and skirting boards flawlessly painted.

Can it?

Unless such a wonder hits the market, I'm condemned to the old-fashioned method, short of swallowing my pride and paying someone else to do it.

My skirmishes with decorating down the years add up to a saga of unparalleled cackhandedness, and one thing the latest episode – a fairly simple paint job in eldest son's bedroom – has demonstrated, yet again, is my poor spatial awareness.

I've always been prone to attack by inanimate objects. They get in the way of my bodily bits.

After years of replacing stained carpets, I've managed to kick the habit of leaving cups of tea and glasses of wine on the floor so that I can toe-end them moments later.

Painful experience has taught me the folly of leaving a drawer open while fixing a cupboard below it, or sawing wood on my knee or unscrewing screws with my fingers.

Nevertheless, I'm forever grazing the same bit of thigh on the corner of the desk I sit at every working day and even though my bathroom cabinet has been in the same position for years, I struggle to clean my teeth without crashing my head against it.

My condition led to an injury that will outlive all other memories of our first holiday abroad without the kids.

It's up there with the time I caught my toe on a step and went sprawling as we hurried back to our flat in Greece, resulting in an hour-long sulk during which no one dared speak to Dad, until Mum could stand it no longer and almost had a bladder accident laughing.

This time, ten days in Gibraltar allowed us to do very little but eat, drink and try not to worry that our home-alone teenager might throw a party that disturbed the neighbours into the early hours.

We soaked up the sunshine and spectacular scenery, learned a little of the Rock and its place in battles down the centuries, visited its famous tunnels and glimpsed its even more famous apes, which, despite signs urging tourists not to feed them, are now venturing into the city, having developed a taste for crisps and Opal Fruits.

But what I learnt above all is that heated towel rails are more dangerous than mosquitoes. This is a pity because the joy of stepping straight from hot shower to hot towel is something my radiator at home has never been equal to.

One evening, having enjoyed this little luxury in our holiday apartment, I was standing naked in the bathroom when I heard the unmistakable buzz of a mosquito and spotted it dancing around the window. I grabbed a towel and went for the blighter.

Then, victorious, I bent to pick up my shorts – and backed on to the heated towel rail.

Suddenly, the horrors of DIY seemed like a walk in the park as my buttocks met hot metal, producing a squeal that belied my age and gender and left a four-inch scar shaped like jointed piping.

Anarchy in the car park

IT was only a parking spot and I was only a few minutes late. But I just had to make a meal of it.

It's because I'm not a morning person. And I'd had too much sleep – eight hours with barely an interruption, instead of the fitful six that seems a common curse of getting old.

I'd spent a thick-headed hour getting ready for work, during which I'd cut myself shaving, such that it would have floored a normal person, and…

OK, I'll come clean: I've become addicted to grumpiness.

I used to be a nice, laid-back person. Then I had the idea of writing a newspaper column as a grumpy old man and I've grown into a caricature of myself.

Ever noticed how old people do that? They dress strangely or have annoying little habits and when you're young and compassionate, you think: I ought to tell them to make a little change to their dress or mannerisms and they'd be eternally grateful because people would think better of them.

But you don't, of course, and it's too late once you've developed annoying traits yourself, since the target of your attentions would say, 'You're a fine one to talk. Looked in the mirror lately, have we?'

But this is to digress.

I'd arrived at the works car park to find my space taken. I was also running late, but at least I had my fifth limb – that thing I said I'd never rely on like all the other saddos: my mobile phone.

A quick call to the office set in train a full-scale inquiry and, ten minutes later, a young man approached the offending vehicle.

He looked slightly bemused and nodded apologetically. But that was not enough. An old grump's spleen serves only one purpose: to be vented. Words had to be had.

I suppose if he'd come to my window and grovelled, he might have escaped unscathed and we'd have laughed about it next time we passed in a corridor, but I was compelled by an irresistible, and pathetic, urge to make my point, as if being right isn't enough unless it's acknowledged as such by whichever adversary happens to cross my path.

Besides, he was much younger than me and perhaps thought I was important because I was wearing a suit.

With a gritted-teeth 'please', I asked him to hurry up and move his car, at which point he made a fatal mistake: he tried to explain himself. Someone had parked in his space, he said, so he'd taken mine because it was empty.

Nice people draw a line at this point, but not I. 'That's a fine excuse,' I said, 'if we all did that, there'd be…'

And then I said it, '…anarchy.'

I can't believe how stupid I must have sounded.

Anarchy? I used to read books about that when I was his age. It was about a passion for personal freedom and lack of authority.

Not parking spaces.

Finally, having taken my rightful place and watched with malicious glee as the young man squeezed into his new, extremely tight spot, I spent the day feeling thick-headed, nursing a cut chin and knowing that I'd grown slightly more ridiculous, while he no doubt amused his workmates with the tale of the car park nutter.

I'd like to say to him publicly: I'm sorry. And if you ever meet me in a dark alley, just remember that you're much bigger than me.

Cheque out my cookbook

I'VE been having hours of fun with an old recipe book, so much so that I ended up bent double and laughing out loud in a near-deserted car park.

'An old recipe book' hardly does it justice. It's the *Be-Ro Book of Self Raising and Plain Flour Home Recipes*, 34th edition.

I'd almost forgotten it existed but somehow it had survived periodic culls of my bookcase and, as retirement and lockdown conspired to fill my days with idleness, I stumbled across it and rediscovered the appeal that had made it a household favourite when I was a boy.

My love affair with cooking had waned considerably in that time. Countless celebrity recipe books had come and gone, consigned to the charity shop out of frustration over tortuous recipes that required a week's grocery spend to acquire a multitude of ingredients.

The beauty of the Be-Ro book is its simplicity. Only a few basic ingredients are needed and if you follow the recipes, you can't go wrong.

I discovered that the book grew out of the wholesale grocery empire set up in Newcastle in 1880 by Thomas Bell. His top-selling brands included Bells Royal self-raising flour but after the death of Edward VII, it became illegal to use the Royal name, and Bell combined the first two letters to make Be-Ro.

Self-raising flour was more expensive than plain and was regarded as something of a novelty. Bells set out to change this by staging staged a series of exhibition to promote self-raising flour, selling freshly baked cakes and scones to visitors for a shilling. Demand for the recipes was so great that the Be-Ro book was born, designed to help feed hungry families on a low budget.

Eighty pages long, little bigger than an iPhone and now in its 41st edition, it has sold more than 40 million copies. My battered copy has recently spawned a range of small cakes and biscuits that have gone down a storm with children and grandchildren.

But back to my car park episode.

I'd been making biscuits, with the Be-Ro book open. Nearby sat my cheque book, a reminder that I had to pay in a cheque at the building society.

Biscuits baked and sampled, I drove into town, strode towards the building society, felt in my jacket pocket and realised I'd left the cheque book at home.

But never mind: the office was open for another 15 minutes, so I dashed back home, returned to the car park, felt in my pocket for the cheque book – and pulled out the Be-Ro book.

Waiter, there's bread in my handbag

IT had been an odd day even before the incident at the restaurant.

Having nagged two carefree, scampering grandchildren about the need to play safely during a delightful hour on the park, it was me who ended up on his face, clutching a gashed scalp from walking into the unflinching bough of a tree.

Sadly, it failed to clear my head of the fuzziness that had produced some frustrating conversations recently, with my wife and I suffering from bunged-up ears after the clinging cold bug that has been doing the rounds.

Bumbling through between ourselves with such an affliction is one thing; conversing with strangers is quite another, and as we arrived at a little Italian restaurant, we realised we'd made matters worse by forgetting our glasses. Again.

Luckily, our youngest son had joined us and his healthy eyes guided us through the menus that we held, squinting, with outstretched arms.

We were soon enjoying a splendid meal but were only a few mouthfuls in when one of those 'it could only happen to me' moments happened.

As I attempted to cut through a bed of posh toast topped with spicy meat and prawns, a chunk of brittle crust snapped, shot off my plate, cleared a foot or so of table and landed in a half-open handbag hanging from a seat occupied by a lady diner at neighbouring table.

I watched it fly. I watched it land. I could see it sitting clean on top of whatever item was nearest the opening of the bag.

As challenges go this was virgin territory.

The diner had her back to me and was blissfully unaware of what had happened. Should I tell her, or pretend nothing had happened and leave her to discover an unwanted souvenir when she reached for her purse?

Why make a scene when neither bread nor bag had come to harm?

So, swiftly and quietly, I reached into the bag, plucked out the lump of bruschetta and placed it beside my plate. My wife giggled into her hand. Our son rolled his eyes.

We left much later, confident that no one beyond our table had witnessed the incident. I just hope that if there's a purse thief at large, the restaurant staff don't check their CCTV.

Grappling with plastic

I'M bent double over a Marks and Sparks cottage pie, nostrils brushing against potato, teeth nibbling furiously around the edges, and it's not even been cooked yet.

This is what the food packaging zealots have reduced me to.

'Remove film' the box says. It's only a thin piece of plastic. Easy, eh? Is it 'eck as like!

I've managed to grip the few millimetres overhanging one edge of the foil tray and, in trying to peel it off, have created a triangular slit into which I've inserted two fingers in the hope that it might come away in one or two large sections.

Instead I get a dozen slivers, leaving me with a few fragments clinging stubbornly to the edges of the tray. All I can do to avoid cottage pie à la plastic for dinner is to grab at them with my front teeth.

At some time in my life, without fanfare, someone decided that wrapping food to maintain its flavour and keep it safe to eat was not sufficient. It had to be a Berlin Wall against the hungry. Why is it so damned difficult to get at?

The world's strongest man can lift a half-ton weight but I'd challenge him to pull open the wrapper on a packet of Tesco crumpets.

I'd begun to wonder if this was an age thing – something else to rob us of our marbles.

But considerably younger friends and acquaintances shared their plastic nightmares.

'Bacon,' said one. 'It's meant to be re-sealable and you just have to pull the "lift here" tab. But it splits and you have to put the bacon plus the left-over packaging in a sandwich bag to keep it airtight. More plastic!'

'Those "re-sealable" blocks of cheese,' fumed another. 'Unless you have a surgeon's precision, they either don't open at all or refuse to re-seal.'

Then there's chocolate. Bags of giant Buttons are labelled 're-sealable'. In other words, the only way to get at them is to tear off a huge corner, which leads to consuming the contents by the handful.

Nor is it just food for humans. 'Don't talk to me about cat food pouches!' said one friend. 'They have a little cut in the side for easy opening. Try that and see if you don't get cat food down your fingernails first thing in the morning.'

It wouldn't be so bad if these things didn't look so easy to open. If plastic film looked like barbed wire, I'd have no complaints.

And just when you decide that the only way to get into a package is to give it some wellie, what happens?

You end up with rice or pasta exploding on to the floor and have to decant it into a tub or a bag – made of plastic!

Demise of the divan

MY local council has adopted a very sensible policy of collecting bulky household waste free of charge and I'm about to take advantage of it.

In doing so I will complete a tale entitled The Great Divan Debacle in the Pete Pheasant Annals of Domestic Stupidity.

The story began when I learnt that my sister was planning to spend a few days with us. This meant we had to buy a bed for the spare room. The timetable was tight but even I could manage such a task on my own.

'Don't get a divan,' my wife warned me as I set off for the shops. She's logical, you see. She knew a divan would never go up our steep, dog-legged staircase.

But I bought a divan. It was cheap and I could tell by looking at it that it would fit.

It was swiftly delivered and I set about getting I upstairs.

Three hours of heaving, sweating and Olympic-standard swearing later, the wretched thing was wedged two steps from the landing, refusing to budge another inch.

I could picture my wife's face. I knew exactly what she'd say when she arrived home from work.

I turned in desperation to a joiner friend, who quickly arrived with tools and knowhow, subjected me to much-deserved ridicule and took the only possible action to get bed into bedroom: he cleaved off the door surrounds.

This might help to explain why, when it came to getting rid of the wretched bed some years later, the thought of trying to get it downstairs in one piece never entered my head. It had to be dismantled in situ.

I'm sure my joiner friend would have the perfect saw for such an occasion, whereas saws and me are sure to end in sores. But I was not going to be a big wuss again and call for help. Instead, I began dismantling it in my own way, which meant slashing it repeatedly with a Stanley knife and thrashing it to bits with a small hammer.

It put up a good fight. Cheap-tat furniture it might have been but it was a masterpiece of modern construction, with its frame of low-grade timber held rigid by thick, taught fabric and hundreds of hideously sharp pins and staples.

There were splinters. There was sweat. There were a few choice words.

Finally, I carried the shattered frame downstairs in triumph (wearing gardener's gloves to protect my office wallah's delicate hands, of course) and dumped it on the back yard…only to learn later that the council insists that bulky waste must be left in front of the house for collection. In our case, that meant on the pavement, and since collections can be any time from 7am, I'd have to leave the divan's splintered skeleton, plus mattress, in full view of the local populace for a whole night, giving a hillbilly air to the neighbourhood.

I'm pleased that no passersby were injured tripping over or falling on the jagged mess but a little disappointed that I haven't won a Turner Prize for street art.

TV TIMES

In the beginning (and end) was A

AMONG the world's wonders is one that might have passed you by. It involves a group of countries marked by the sort of linguistic quirkiness that appeals to words nerds like me.

My discovery stems from a passion for TV quiz shows that commonly afflicts people of advanced years. We have a strange compulsion to fill our heads with knowledge, even though we are too old to make much use of it.

I particularly enjoy *Pointless* and record it so that I can skip through the boring bits as I savour the TV equivalent of cocoa at bedtime. Not satisfied with trying to answer the questions, I'm prone to declaring how many points I think the contestants will score and have been known to punch the air in triumph when I'm spot-on.

If that's not enough to make you pity my wife as she tries to have a power nap on the sofa beside me, consider this: I once foretold the future, by announcing what the next category of questions would be before it had been revealed on screen.

'How… what?' she gaped. 'How did you know that?' At which point I confessed that I'd rewound the show as she dozed, then nudged her awake.

But back to that group of countries. It was during a question about famous philosophers and their places of origin that Australia and Algeria emerged as answers, and the quizmasters seemed surprised by the number of countries whose name both began and ended with the letter 'a'.

This had never crossed my mind – a short journey, it must be said – but it kept me awake that night and before long, I dug out my atlas and settled down for some serious research, armed with pen and jotter. The results were a-mazing. As well as Australia and Algeria, there's Albania, Andorra, Angola, Argentina, Armenia, Austria, and Antigua and Barbuda – nine out of 11 countries, or 81.8 per cent – the exceptions being Afghanistan and Azerbaijan

I wouldn't be half as excited if this pattern applied to other letters of the alphabet but, as my jottings show, out of 190 nations, only six have the same letter at the start and end of their names. There's one among the 18 'c' countries – the Czech

Republic. That's a measly 5.5 per cent. And though 26 countries begin with an 's', only four (15.3 per cent) also end with one: St Kitts and St Nevis, St Vincent and the Grenadines, Seychelles and the Solomon Islands.

Why, oh why, is 'a' so different? If it wasn't for the fact that those nine nations evolved independently over thousands of years, I might think a World Naming Council was secretly at work.

I revealed the fruits of my research to my son. 'Don't you think it's weird?' I asked.

'It is,' he said with a smirk, 'but not half as weird as you making a chart out of it.'

Continuity murder in Midsomer

BEING of an age where losing the plot is all too familiar, I can do very well without the help of TV programme makers – but one episode of *Midsomer Murders* threw me into a spin.

I'd never gone much for whodunnits but had found *Midsomer* a reasonable way to pass a couple of hours of an evening. For the uninitiated, the series centres on a policeman – Detective Chief Inspector Barnaby – whose patch is a cluster of sleepy English villages that throw up an extraordinary number of multiple murders without the press seemingly ever getting wind of crimes that would normally make page one of *The Sun*.

Two Barnabys on the same side – but it wasn't always the case.

I can suspend my disbelief on that score, however. I also managed to get my head around the fact that DCI Barnaby is not the man he used to be. For 14 years, the role of Tom Barnaby was played by John Nettles. Subsequently, Neil Dudgeon appeared as John Barnaby. A bit odd them having the same name, you might think? Ah well, Tom is John's younger cousin. But the same rank and the same area to police? Yes, I know, it stretches credibility a little, but let's move on.

The plots are brilliantly tortuous and never an episode passes without me pressing 'pause' on the remote control to quiz the missus over who this, that or the other character is. Such are the joys of domestic life at Chez Phez.

Since we have these programmes on record, it's not unusual for us to watch one from, say, 20 years ago one evening and five years ago on another. Even I can understand that DCI Tom retired and DCI John took over. But while watching an early episode this week, a dodgy character looked very familiar. And then I twigged: it was DCI John, as he would later become – not playing DCI Tom's younger cousin, but totally unrelated to him. And not only was he an oily lothario quite unfit to become a senior copper, he was making a play for the old DCI's wife!

Yes, I understand they're not real characters. I also accept that, in a long-running show that attracts some seriously good actors, the same faces will pop up from time to time in different roles.

But dodgy geezer to top cop is a serious crime by the continuity department.

And all this came within days of serious befuddlement entirely of my own making when, on arriving late at my son's cricket match, I greeted his early strokes with shouts of 'well played, Dan' and even signalled that I'd brought along his water bottle, as asked … only to be confronted by him moments later, padded up, waiting to go in and wondering why I was applauding his team-mate.

EastEnders' gross grannie

I HAVE endured many indignities from Britain's most popular TV soap but the Grannie Who Needs A Wee is one tick too many on the *EastEnders* diversity list.

The show's creators bend over backwards to be inclusive, showcasing ethnic minorities and all manner of social and health problems in stories of murder, deceit and fractured love lives that make Albert Square the misery capital of the UK.

There are tales to make the most tortured lives of viewers seem like a bed of roses by comparison. As I write…

The local councillor has vanished after being poisoned by a friend whose son he left to drown at a boat party.

The convicted killer son of the square's gangster-in-chief (three times married, seven lovers, three children, one of whom tried to shoot him dead) is set to marry a gay police officer.

One of the Square's many 'maaafy cows' is behind bars, wrongly accused of causing another to have a miscarriage by pushing her downstairs. The prisoner's lawyer has got away with beating his wife to death, strangling the bisexual client he framed for a crime and throwing a 'grass' under a train.

The mother of a Down's Syndrome girl is in love with the young man her ex-husband treated as a son.

An undertaker is trying to find someone to hire as a surrogate mum, a schoolgirl has run away from home rather than burden her hard-up dad, and a bipolar neighbour is dying of cancer.

A woman who gave her son up for adoption has him back after the adoptive parents died in a car crash and the old West Indian gent she thought was her father has a son with schizophrenia.

The local publican is married to an alcoholic. He's discovered the (deaf) daughter whose existence had been kept a secret by the social worker who abused him as a child.

And a Sikh mum who sent her son to prison with her lies because she disapproved of his girlfriend has since slept with the boyfriend of her daughter, who'd previously had a relationship with a lesbian Muslim.

Hardly surprising that there's no room on the scriptwriters' inclusivity list for that cultural oddity, the happy heterosexual couple with two children born in wedlock.

I can forgive them for all of the above, and more. But did they really have to introduce a bladder-busting old lady on primetime TV?

The grannie had only just turned up at the gay cop's home when she headed for the loo, saying, 'I need to wet my lettuce, that coffee's gone straight through me.'

And when she returned it was with the news that 'you can't beat three-ply, it's like being tickled with a feather'.

Ew. I can do without that over my TV dinner.

SORT-OF POLITICS

Changing the faces of Britain

THERE follows a party political broadcast by the Change The Face Of Britain Party.

'Good evening.

'Everyone's talking about change. But for most politicians, that's all it is – talk. I want to tell you how we can make a real difference to our society. We intend to change the face of Britain, literally.

'You don't have to be a genius to realise that there is vast inequality in our country and that this is at the root of many social problems.

'Many people have nowhere near enough money, while others have far too much. Some – and there's not a nice way to say this – are not particularly bright, while others are too clever by half. Many are not very nice to look at, while others are far too pretty.

'As these different types continue in their own little worlds, so the inequality grows.

'We need to be honest with ourselves if we are ever to make society a fairer place. For example, have you never observed a member of the idle rich, stunningly good looking, dressed in the finest clothes, dripping with expensive jewellery, driving to their beautiful house in a flash car loaded with fresh fruit and veg from their weekly shop and thought, "That's not fair. I should be like that. He/she shouldn't have all that wealth. I should have some – or they should share it with poor people in Africa"?

'I suspect you've also come across poor people who were evidently beaten at birth with the Ugly Stick, who are unwashed, overweight and spotty from eating junk food because that's all they can afford and who seem unable to speak without swearing VERY LOUDLY.

'If you have a dreg of compassion, I bet you've thought, "That's not fair either; there's enough wealth and cleverness for everyone but some poor souls don't stand a chance of breaking their chains and going up in the world. Wouldn't it be nice if we could bring these diverse people together?"

'It would indeed, dear voter, which is why we have come up with a programme of radical equalisation. This will encourage people from opposite ends of the social spectrum to pair up. As a result of voluntary cross-breeding, some of the more unpleasant characteristics on both sides will gradually be removed.

'Just think how much nicer the world would be if there were fewer hairy-faced ladies with enormous backsides barely covered by grubby tracksuit bottoms, and fewer suntanned I'm-all-right-Jack types with perfect teeth and 4x4s.

'Put these people together and the result will be quieter neighbourhoods, less crime, more tolerance and fewer road accidents as a result of a reduction in tooth dazzle.

'Obviously, we can't expect either side to make such a leap from their comfort zone without an incentive, which is why we will offer generous tax breaks to those willing to marry above or below their station.

'Citizens' panels will be formed to assess the size of the social divide, based on various indicators of wealth and deprivation, and approved couples will be given a year's honeymoon from income tax payments.

'We will appoint inspectors to ensure the rough edges are indeed being smoothed out and not merely put side by side. The last thing we want is some suntanned, blinged-up businessman in a hoodie, thrashing a Porsche around a council estate while swigging chardonnay.

'As with any major programme of social engineering, there are risks – but imagine the change we could bring about in a few short years.

'We will also increase spending on health, the police and education, abolish VAT and bring back some good old British values, starting with the introduction of free custard for the under-eights.

'So, don't let the three big parties tell you there's no alternatives to the tired, old political system. Vote for prettier faces on May the sixth.'

Seven portions for MPs

THE Prime Minister said he wished to address the House on a matter of national importance.

'I believe it is our duty,' he said, 'to set a lead in the battle against cancer, heart disease and obesity. I therefore intend to bring before this House emergency legislation requiring honourable members to eat seven portions of fruit and vegetables per day.'

(Shouts of 'shame')

'Quiet, please, quiet! My honourable friends, it is pure hypocrisy for Parliament to implore the population to eat healthily if MPs themselves are not willing to set an example. I therefore propose sweeping changes in the members' restaurants. Out with belly pork and in with brassicas! Down with pies, in with peaches!'

(Groans)

'Furthermore, each member shall be issued with a check-card so that his or her daily intake of fruit and veg can be monitored. Anyone falling below the required standard more than once in a week shall be temporarily suspended from this House.'

(Stunned silence, followed by much flapping of papers)

'You're treating us like children, Prime Minister!' yelled one MP. 'And where's this seven portions nonsense come from? It used to be five.'

'And why should we trust the Food Police?' said another honourable member. 'They're forever changing their minds.'

'They used to tell us eggs and cheese and butter were good for us,' cried a third. 'Then someone invented cholesterol. First it was "fat will kill you". Now it's sugar.

'And who really knows what constitutes a portion?'

'It's all on the NHS website,' said the Health Secretary. 'One banana's a portion. So is a handful of grapes, three tablespoons of baked beans, two florets of broccoli.'

'Big handfuls or little handfuls?' came a cry from the back benches.

'Red grapes or green grapes?'

'I hate broccoli!' wailed a cut-glass voice. 'Nanny used to mix it in one's mashed potatoes.'

'Does a Chocolate Orange count as fruit?'

'Or tomato sauce?'

The heaving figure of the Minister for Fat People rose to his feet. 'I'm afraid I must disagree with my friend the Prime Minister on this occasion…

(Shouts of 'who's a brave little piggy?')

'…because,' the minister continued, 'all of us have, in our constituencies, a large number of people who do not follow a healthy diet and it is surely our duty to reflect all strands of society.'

(Cries of 'rhubarb')

'I therefore suggest that MPs continue to eat meat, pastries, cakes, custards, etc, if they so wish.'

(Cries of 'custard')

'What about fish?' asked the Ukipper leader.

'And leek smoothies,' came a lilting Welsh voice.

'MPs will still be able to eat unhealthy food,' the Health Secretary yelled above the hubbub, 'so long as they offset this by eating more than seven portions of fruit and veg.

'I have done some preliminary calculations and a sausage butty, for example, would require the consumption of a handful of cherry tomatoes, or equivalent. However, I propose a working party to establish a full tariff of offences and reparations.'

'Count me in,' cried the Minister for Fat People. 'As long as there's tea and biscuits.'

'Oh, shut up, round boy,' said the Prime Minister.

MPs will vote on the Sausage Amendment next week.

The War on Filth

CELEBRITY sex scandals are dominating the news once more and deep in the bowels of Westminster, a bemused civil servant knocks on an unfamiliar door. The sign reads 'Control of Ogling and Inappropriate Touching, Undergarments and Speech'.

'Come!' booms a voice from within. 'Er, I mean, enter... er, oh do step inside.'

'Ah, Poppleton,' says a fat man with a thin smile. 'Just the chap. You have been highly recommended as someone who can cut through red tape and get a job done.'

'Why, thank you, Minister.'

'Now, I want you to take on a project of the utmost importance: a national crusade. You must have seen the news, Poppleton. Politicians and film stars being dobbed in for indiscretions from years ago. Hands on knees, slaps on bottoms, lewd remarks, coming outs, staying in. Accusations. Confessions. They're all at it.'

'At what, Minister?'

'Filth, Poppleton, filth! Well, we're not going to put up with it. We're going to make this country clean and wholesome once more, starting with books.

'We – that is, you – are going to see to it that every book on sale is renamed so as to avoid even a grain of double meaning, sexual activity or gender discrimination in its title. Starting with the Dic... er, the Book of Word Definitions.'

Poppleton retrieves his lower jaw. 'But...'

'Yes, what is it, man? Spit it out – in a hankie, if you please.'

'What you're asking is impossible, Minister. It's such a huge undertaking.'

'Indeed it is, Poppleton – but nothing's impossible, not where there's a wi... a desi... er, a determination.'

'But what about the cost?'

The minister leans forward and whispers, 'Cost is no object, Poppleton. This comes from the very top.'

'You mean Number 10.'

'Higher.'

'The Quee...'

'Ahem, not a word we like, Poppleton. We prefer "sovereign". Now, I have a few ideas to get you started. See if you can guess what the titles of these books were before I had a little play with them:

'*A Young Person's Adventures in Wonderland.*

'*Sons and Acquaintances.*

'*Winnie the Woodland Creature.*

'*Noddy and His Friend With Normal-sized Ears.*

'*Of Mice And Persons.*'

The Minister sits back with a satisfied smile. 'Not bad, eh, Poppleton?'

The civil servant looks askance.

'But I'm sure you can do better. Now, get back to me in 48 hours with an action plan. And if you think our policy on books is radical, what I'm about to show you is strictly for your eyes only. It will be the next stage in our clean-up campaign, the ace in the pack as it were.'

He opens a cupboard to reveal coat hangers from which dangle an assortment of transparent full-body suits, fitted with tubes, dials and switches.

'I give you Innocence!' the minister beams. 'This invention has been years in the making, Poppleton. We intend to fit one of these to every person in the land.'

'To what, erm, end, Minister?'

'Simple! It will allow one to do everything one needs and stop one doing anything one shouldn't. All bodily functions are catered for within these extraordinary suits, so there need be no unpleasant emissions or extrusions. No need even to undress. There's even a voice controller that scans what one says and replaces rude words with nice ones.

'Say "goodbye" to scandals and rudeness, Poppleton!'

'But what about children, Minister? Won't people be able to have, erm, you know, inter…'

'Interpersonal relations? Of course, man… er, colleague. We're not monsters, you know. However, such congress will have to be authorised and a licence obtained from the relevant department, specifying time, place, partner, purpose and duration of activity.'

The civil servant turns, dazed, to leave.

'And Poppleton,' says the Minister, 'have that sign removed from my door, would you? I've just noticed those initials – C.O.I.T.U.S.'

Persons of a gingerbread disposition

A SMALL bakery in a city suburb was the last place I expected to witness political correctness gone mad.

But among the rows of caramel shortbreads and custard tarts were the familiar delicacies I planned to buy for my grandsons – with a label that read 'Gingerbread Person'.

'Two gingerbread MEN, please,' I said firmly, drawing an amused glance from a shop assistant of advanced years.

I soon found myself trying to rewrite the traditional nursery story, but with some difficulty, since there's hardly another word in the English language that rhymes with 'person'. The best I could manage was:

Run, run, I bet you daresn't
You'll never catch me,
I'm the Gingerbread Person.

But it couldn't stop there, of course. The whole story would need reworking.

I'd start with the old woman. Putting one's child in an oven is bad enough but then to allow it to escape and run away at such a tender age must surely attract the attention of Social Services.

She's already in trouble for insisting on milk chocolate for the eyes, nose and shirt buttons, much to the dismay of White Chocolate Matters.

Her gingerbread child has only just got down the lane when he's menaced by a cow and a horse that think he'd make a good meal. I trust they'll be outed on social media by the vegan brigade.

Then comes Mr Fox. He should be prosecuted under the Fraud Act for attempting to obtain a dietary advantage by deception. All that 'I'll get you across the stream safely, climb on my back/grab my tail/sit on my nose' malarkey shows that the final outrage was premeditated.

But Mr Fox is destined to suffer before the case gets to court, for while that buttery gingerbread body tastes great going down, it contains flour – and after a few days of feeling tired and itchy, he's diagnosed with coeliac disease.

Now, he's launching an online campaign for better food labelling.

DOMESTIC BLISS

Our bedtime soap opera

'WHAT on earth,' I spluttered as I stretched full out and found my foot resting against something hard and waxy, 'is a bar of soap doing in our bed?'

'I saw something on the internet,' my wife laughed.

Oh, here we go, I thought.

'It's supposed to be good for bad legs,' she said.

'What a load of old tosh! How?'

'I dunno. Some people said it had done them good, so I thought it was worth a try. For your leg.'

'My leg', which happens to be one of a pair, aches from thigh to calf when I lie down. It's from a back injury I suffered a few years ago when I (stupidly) carried a pushchair, laden with grandson, down several steep steps while bent double. As a result, I spend the first hour or so in bed tossing, turning, bending and stretching while I suspect my wife's silently screaming, 'FOR HEAVEN'S SAKE, STOP FIDGETING!'

I'm forever taking the mickey out of old wives' tales, superstitions and any suggestion that mystical powers might be at work and yet here I was being asked to place at least a grain of faith in a bar of soap.

I've had physiotherapy on my leg. I've worked it in the gym. I swim and do daily stretching exercises and still it aches at night. So, what will a bar of Dove Original do? Wait until I finally succumb to sleep, then release the Soap Fairy to wash away the naughty pain?

And yet... I can barely bring myself to utter the words... it's as if my whole outlook on life has been turned upside-down... and yet: I have not suffered night-time leg ache for two weeks. Ever since the soap slipped between the sheets. And this cannot be down to the placebo effect because I was ache-free for two nights while the soap, unbeknown to me, was sharing our sheets.

I turned to the internet, hoping to make sense of this madness. Sure enough, there were several posts by people claiming that a bar of fresh soap in the bed cured 'restless leg syndrome', but it had to be lavender-scented, they said – and placed *beneath* the bottom sheet. Neither applied in our case, so it's just faintly, ridiculously possible that my missus has stumbled upon a great medical advance.

But let's be sensible: my 'cure' is down to coincidence. It must be. Whatever caused the ache just happened to disappear, for good physiological reasons, on the same day as the coming of the soap. Either that or I fell asleep straight away on those first two nights and promptly got out of the habit of being restless as soon as I climbed into bed.

No other explanation will wash, surely?

A world of dirt and danger

I'VE been to a dark place and come out the other side.

Allow me to set the scene: day off work, house to myself, no must-do jobs to be done.

I can laze about, unwashed and unshaven, reading the paper, watching TV, feasting on tea and biscuits.

Or I can stop being a sad, stereotypical bloke and Do Something Useful – aaargh, the words won't stop coming! – Around The House.

I mop my brow and pinch myself: no, I'm not dreaming.

When I say 'no must-do jobs to be done', I mean the man-of-the-house variety, which excludes ironing, washing, dusting, putting clothes away, shopping, cleaning windows and minor electrical and plumbing work, for all of which I have a perfectly competent wife.

So, what chore shall I tackle? It has to be something that won't deprive the lady of the house of job satisfaction; something she doesn't enjoy doing. Mmm, difficult.

Tea. Biscuits. Deep breaths.

I've decided: I'll de-crud the hole where the cooker sits.

Despite the absence of safety suit and rubber gloves (note to self: remind the better half of her responsibilities vis a vis health and safety), I set to work, twisting the cooker this way and that to ease it out – and trapping my hand between cooker and cupboard. Fffflip, that hurt!

The gunk down here is unbelievable: caked-on rivers and pimples of grease, a few hairs, a pasta spiral, two raisins and a new species of fluff.

This would never have happened years ago. They'd have wiped up the gunk with a slice of bread and fed it to Grannie for her supper. That's why the wartime generation's so 'ard.

Out comes the hoover and I spend ages disconnecting the hose and finding somewhere to slot it into, then taking one nozzle out of another out of another. It's like a Russian doll. And still it won't work, even though I've cunningly located the on/off switch. Ah yes: it's not plugged in.

Bowl of water and scouring pad at the ready, it's time to choose my cleaning fluid. I snub the one that goes with a flash in favour of the one that boasts a bang, despite the horrifying safety instructions (do not gargle, snort, spray in eyes, bathe in – that sort of thing).

There follows much frantic fiddling for the 'on' bit of the spray nozzle, because it's the same colour as the rest of the bottle. Don't they give a thought to squinting old buffoons when they design these things?

A hairy spider, a foot wide if it's an inch, squeezes out from behind the cupboard and as I recoil, my elbow meets some of the fluid that's supposedly eating its way into the grime. Now I bet I'll lose an arm.

Feverish, I read the instructions once more, 'Do not leave on enamel surfaces for more than five minutes.' Now they tell me. Still, if I get a move on and put the cooker back, the missus might never notice that the sides have disintegrated.

It seems like weeks have passed but it's little more than half an hour. Gunk and grease have all gone. Floor spotless.

All that remains is to disconnect the hoover and curse the invisible fiend who's tied the cable in a knot, the same one who steals my cutlery, eats my pens and hides my glasses in the most bizarre places.

I stand back to admire my work, arms raised in triumph to the adulation of an unseen crowd, and think: this housework lark's a doddle.

The author of clutter

ONE of the most enduring writers of mankind's rich story has been busy in my life of late.

This author has been causing clutter in the tidy lives of men and women for as long as they've had more possessions than they know what to do with.

I refer, of course, to Justin Case.

His works have kept my wardrobe cluttered for decades. *The Chronicles Of The Tatty T-shirts* features more than a dozen characters long past their fit-to-go-out-in days but kept, limp and creased, just in case they come in useful one day.

My missus owns the chick-lit version: *Skimpy Dresses Wot I Used To Fit Into*.

Rummaging in a drawer for something I needed, I completely forgot what it was, thanks to the web of confusion spun by Justin Case storylines involving, among others, a piece of string, a shoelace from shoes long discarded, electrical leads for goodness knows what, a bagful of door knobs removed because they were old and ugly (but one day, who knows?), a padlock without a key and a gift tag awaiting marriage to one of the scraps of leftover wrapping paper gathering dust beneath my bed.

You might have come across these works by the inimitable Mr Case:

- *A Fistful Of Pre-decimal Coins* (That Will Surely Be Worth A Fortune One Day)
- *Charge Of The Phone Chargers For Lost Phones*
- *1984* (Was When This Battery Last Worked)
- *Silence Of The Jams: The Forgotten Ones*
- *The Broken Time Machine*
- And who could forget *Paint Your Wagon (If You Can Get The Top Off That Tin With Half An Inch Of Rubbery Stuff Inside)*?

There's no doubt that Mr Case can be a force for good: I, for instance, have resisted the idea of sending my old spectacles to poor people in the Third World so that I can have fun trying to find them when my new ones go missing.

Some people, however, are hopelessly addicted to preparing for 'a rainy day'. TV programmes like *Britain's Biggest Hoarders* reveal the true fanatics.

And then there are those like my old friend John. Nothing goes to the tip unless it's been stripped of anything that might be useful.

TVs, computers, doors – you name it, John will take out every last screw, hinge and handle. And if you dare suggest that by doing so, he's denying someone else the prospect of making use of one of his discarded appliances, he'll snort, 'Why should *they* have something for nowt? *I* paid for it!'

I can't be as meticulous as John. I tend to wait until the bookshelves of my brain are heaving, then I turn to an old remedy: charity shops, which now not only welcome all those CDs containing just one good track, and the wig you once wore to a fancy dress party, but write to you afterwards, saying how much they've made from selling your unwanted items to other tat collectors.

Good job there's no market for the hundreds of notes and half-baked ramblings I've amassed over the years. With a newspaper column to write, I keep those just in…

Things that go boing in the night

I'VE been having trouble with Tigger. Not the cartoon version of Winnie the Pooh's pal who boings around on his tail shouting 'Hello, buddy boy!' but a soft toy lookalike that's quietly occupied the same spot in my bedroom for years.

In between visits by young relatives, when's he's fetched down to play, Tigger rests undisturbed for months on end on a pile of old newspapers, scrapbooks and photos vainly awaiting 'filing', on a shelf six feet up a wall above a chest of drawers.

Until one night recently, when my wife awoke with a start because something had fallen on her head.

Out came a few unladylike words, on went the light and there, on the floor beside the bed, was Tigger.

I promptly offered reasonable explanations, like a juggernaut roaring by and shaking the house to its foundations; or a mini earthquake; or an aircraft looking to land on the local park, having lost its way en route to China.

'Or perhaps,' I said, as the missus tried to put the episode out of mind, 'perhaps Tigger jumped.'

'Don't say things like that, you'll spook me!' she huffed.

And therein lies one of the little differences that help to sustain our long marriage, because while she believes in hidden forces – and has experienced several 'supernatural' incidents down the years – I don't and haven't.

Not once have I had a ghostly experience, though I've met many who say they have. Indeed, I was reminded of a story I covered for a local newspaper 30-something years ago when it popped up on a bygones website recently. That's me these days: a bygone.

The landlord of a pub I used to frequent had phoned to say I should get up there sharpish because one of his customers had been driven out of his home by a poltergeist.

I soon found myself interviewing a burly ex-Marine who had seemingly been reduced to a quivering wreck by door handles flying off, his wife's head being forced under water as she took a bath, and plant pots floating through the air.

He appeared utterly genuine, though the cynic in me wondered if it was all a stunt to get the family rehoused. Eventually, however, an exorcism was performed and their life returned to normal.

I have close friends who insist they have contacted dead relatives at psychic sessions and one whose very bright son fled his university digs after apparitions began hovering inches above his face in bed.

I don't doubt their sincerity for a minute but I've never been there myself and I sometimes wonder if that's because I won't open my mind to the possibility.

Can the spirits sense that? Does one need a receptive mind to see the proof, much as with religion, perhaps?

I find life complicated enough with things I can see, touch, smell, taste and hear, without inviting in gods and demons and things that go bump in the night.

Except Tigger. He can stay. But he's been consigned to the spare room.

Don't DIY it

FOR those about to pick up a paint brush, allow me to share a cautionary tale.

I should say at the outset that I practise a peculiar form of DIY known as PIY (Pete It Yourself) in which anything that can go wrong usually does.

The statistics show that I'm far from alone, however. Easter weekend botch jobs alone cost £58m to put right, according to one insurance company, and with a new year resolve to fix things around the house still coursing through the nation's veins, I feel it is a duty to warn those of a similar disposition.

Mine was only a simple paint job: the bathroom boiler cupboard/towel store hid cracked walls and peeling paint. I would seal them with a coat of emulsion.

Suitably shod in carpet slippers, I perched on a small stool, tin of paint in one hand, large slap-it-on brush in the other, and set about the task. This entailed stretching to reach walls and ceiling because, spanning the cupboard doorway about halfway up, is a piece of three-by-two, fixed there to keep the cupboard in shape.

All went well until, for reasons forgotten in the ensuing panic, I stepped down from the stool and, in doing so, clipped the bottom of the paint tin on the piece of three-by-two, tipping half its lilac contents across the bathroom floor.

There was not even time to swear as I bounded downstairs in search of an old washing up bowl and a kitchen roll.

Half an hour later, the mess was all gone – except for flecks of lilac paint in the black grout between the grey ceramic floor tiles. These I later tried to remove with white spirit and fine sandpaper but it was no use: the grout looked a mess.

'Scrape it out and re-grout it,' said a friend, concealing, I suspect, a wicked grin. Never had the words 'you must be joking' been more apt.

Besides, I had a plan.

One visit to a stationery shop later, I was on my knees on the cruel floor, colouring in the grout with a black magic marker, aided by a cheap plastic ruler.

The early results were impressive and I braced myself to tackle the entire floor... until, after a tea break, I noticed that the magic marker had dried, not black, but a shade of bronze. The floor looked worse than ever.

In the hand-wringing debates that followed, I flatly rejected my wife's idea of putting lino down. Then we went shopping for lino.

We even found some we liked and were about to order when the salesman, bless him, asked what kind of surface it would be covering. 'Ah, tiles,' he said. 'You'll need to screed it first – self-levelling compound should do it.'

So, we now have a smart boiler room that no one but me and the missus ever looks inside and a bathroom floor that will take hundreds of pounds to put right.

Time to remember the golden rule of PIY: get a man in.

WILDLIFE

Letter from the Head Wasp

I HAVE received the following communication from Mr S.T. Inger, who describes himself as president of the British Council of Wasps.

'Sir, I was alarmed to read your comments in the local press concerning your experience of being stung by a wasp.

'As the head of Britain's vast wasp population, I must take issue with the arrogant tone of your article.

'Firstly, let me say that wasps are highly intelligent creatures, inhabiting an extremely complex and sophisticated civilisation.

'As with all civilised societies, we have guerrillas in our midst. Those followers of the organisation known as WASP (We Always Sting People) are regarded by the rest of us as hooligans. The vast majority of decent wasps sting only for a purpose.

'Wasps stem from several great families and their highly advanced senses of smell and hearing allow them to communicate over great distances.

'Far from being "random stingers" they will make the pursuit of those who have harmed their loved ones their life's mission.

'However, in many cases, man and wasp come into conflict through a misunderstanding of our intentions. The child licking his ice-cream, for example, has no need to fear the attentions of wasps circling his dessert. They want only to lick and scarper. But, by an amazing coincidence, the childish shriek of "help, mummy!" translates as "get him!" in Ancient Waspish.

'Similarly, the sweet-smelling hair of an old lady on a bus might confuse the less intelligent wasp into believing he has discovered the Great Blue Nest for Lost Souls.

'And the thing you call a litter bin filled with cola cans bears a striking resemblance to the fabled Paradise Tower of Waspish legend.

'When decent wasps sting, it is for a reason: the wafted hand, the flailing newspaper, the cutting verbal abuse.

'In your case, sir, the wasp that "just happened to be there" when you gripped the handlebar of your bicycle was none other than Special Agent Harold H.

"Buzz" Hornet, sole surviving heir of Lady "Bendy" Wendy Waspkinson-Smyth, "it" girl to the royal court.

'As you well know, sir, on one murderous day in 1963, you splattered that fine lady and 30 other innocents with a slipper before stewing them in a jam jar full of water, which you subsequently spilt on your mother's finest tablecloth. And you talk about cruelty!

'But now, at last, "Buzz" is avenged and I hope this proves a salutary lesson to you and the rest of mankind.'

This strange letter left me thinking that perhaps I'd been rather mean to wasps in the past. I was mulling this over when my young son picked up his juice flask at a football match and was stung on the finger. I suppose that particular wasp harboured a grudge because, one day years ago, his great-grandfather's cousin's tennis partner was crushed under the wheels of my son's pushchair.

Well, that does it!

From this day forward the entire wasp population should be advised that a state of war exists between us.

Urgh! I hardly dare look.

Mottephobia and me

IT was midway through a large family gathering at a Chinese restaurant that the pterodactyl appeared. Well, not exactly a dinosaur. A bird, more like.

OK, it was a moth – but what a whopper! Black and at least three feet, or inches, across, it twirled and darted between tables as faces dribbling sweet and sour chicken bobbed and weaved out of its path and feet sprang up lest it should find a way up skirt or trouser leg.

'Get it!' a woman squealed.

'Gone,' said my year-old grandson, arms outstretched in wonder.

And standing a yard or so from his seat, sweat breaking on brow, ready to run for it, was I.

Don't expect any logic on this subject. There's not a shred of reason for my fear of moths. I am, after all, a member of the mightiest, most intelligent species on earth. They are dumb, fluttering things.

I weigh 13 stone compared with their few grams. They have no means of inflicting pain on me – not even the South American white witch moth, with its 11-inch wingspan (though I'd probably need a change of underwear if we met).

But I've had this phobia for as long as I can remember and, even as a young dad, in that period when the sponge-like brains of young children are at their most porous and parents strive to avoid passing on their own anxieties, I was unable to hide the twinge of panic whenever a butterfly with attitude came into view.

I wouldn't mind so much if they'd stay still for a few seconds but all that whirling and dipping, out of sight one minute, around my head the next, make for an unfair fight

And why, you might ask, do I see it as a battle? Why not leave the poor things in peace? They're harmless little marvels of creations, all 160,000 varieties of them, having a bit of fun, trying to survive and taking a close look at me now and then. And all I can think of is 'kill!'

What a great big girl's blouse I am.

That's the thing about phobias, though: they make no sense to other people. But if you think mottephobia (fear of moths) is weird, I once worked with a woman who was afraid of garden peas, and she's not alone, it seems: lachanophobia is the recognised term for an irrational aversion to vegetables.

In fact, you name it and there's probably someone who's terrified of it, from infinity and gold to string and gravity, according to the online Phobia List.

Among the hundreds of recognised panic triggers are Dutch people, the Pope, the act of sitting down, long words, belly buttons, the mother-in-law, heat, chopsticks and laughter.

I couldn't help laughing at the thought of someone with arachibutyrophobia – a morbid fear of peanut butter sticking to the roof of the mouth. But then, he probably keeps moths for a hobby.

Eight-legged terrors

THERE are some whopping spiders about these days. Friends and relatives confirm that I'm not alone in sitting with feet several inches off the floor while watching the telly in case a big, brown intruder comes scuttling out of its hidey hole.

As a child I was taught that there was an old lady who swallowed a fly. I wasn't to know why she swallowed a fly but it was thought she might die. Instead, she swallowed a spider that wriggled and jiggled and tickled inside her – and all to catch the fly. Then came political correctness and, while the humble fly might still be considered fair game for old ladies, spiders seem to have acquired protected-species status.

Perhaps Arachnids Anonymous (introductory confession, 'Hi, I'm Steve/ Mildred and I'm a spider') has been flexing its muscles in the corridors of powers.

Or perhaps old ladies have swallowed so many flies that they've gone loopy and ended up in nursing homes, depriving extended families of their pest control function.

Our resident eight-legged friend reappeared last night and, on hearing our gasps, stood bold as brass, weighing us up. We've named him Eric but my wife tells me there's one even bigger doing the rounds. Apparently, it wears a hoodie and gesticulates rudely at her.

I say 'him' because we're more likely to see the male of the species, since he roams in search of a mate at this time of year. The female will be hiding in her triangular cobweb in a neglected corner, awaiting inquisitive flies.

Eventually, along comes Mr Spider and, after several weeks of 16-legged rumpy pumpy, she has him for dinner – and the nutrients help to feed their offspring.

Now that's what I call child benefit.

With a body of ten to 18mm, the house spider might seem fearsome but it's a baby against the biggest of the world's 40,000 species of arachnids, the Goliath bird-eating spider, which can grow to 4.7in and weigh more than 6oz. Plus legs.

Fear of spiders is one of the hundreds of recorded phobias that afflict our all-conquering species. Johnny Depp might be a hard man on screen but he's a scaredy pants when it comes to spiders. Harry Potter author JK Rowling is another, though it hasn't stopped her filling impressionable young minds with far scarier beasts

It's all very irrational. I mean, it's not as if we're likely to be bitten by spiders, not in this country, are we?

Er, well, the Natural History Museum has reliable accounts of bites by 12 species in the UK, from the tiny money spider ('sewage plant workers bitten by large numbers … resulting in local redness and swelling') to the 15mm false widow ('burning sensation on right side of ribs … like being scalded … stabbing pains spread to armpit and down right arm … flu-like symptoms … face went purplish … unwell for three days').

Then there's Bruennichi's Argiope ('immediate local pain, spreading to the groin'). That's a bit below the belt.

But remember, the crimes featured here are rare, so don't have nightmares.

Incidentally, I got most of this off the web.

Slimy encounters

MY wife has been mugged by a slug.

She'd spent the evening at a wedding reception and was approaching our front door when the beast struck.

I don't know if the maximum speed at which one foot can become parted from the other over the greatest possible distance, while remaining attached to the body, has ever been calculated.

But it's dramatically illustrated when one steps on a slug on a wet pavement.

And so it was that my better half's knee crashed to the ground, causing a graze that would smart for several days, and even such a charitable soul as she could find little consolation in the thought that the slug had come off worse.

I hope this won't sour our view of slugs.

A keen gardener friend detests them for the damage they do to his crops and misses no opportunity to consign them to the great cabbage patch in the sky.

But unless they happen to be hiding on the back of a milk bottle, or glued to a bathroom wall, indicating an urgent need for re-plastering, I've always found them quite fascinating, especially the ones that look like they're made of white chocolate or Caramac – and the shrivelled-up variety which, as *Blackadder*'s Baldrick famously illustrated, make a marvellous Charlie Chaplin moustache.

Did you know, for instance, that the Large Black, native to these shores, can be 20cm long, while Great Greys mate by climbing walls or fences and dangling from a tough rope of mucus, with their genitalia entwined, after which one drops to the ground and the other climbs up the rope, eating it as it goes?

It's difficult not to admire such sexual athleticism, though it's purely out of self-preservation that I tread gingerly at night during spells of wet weather that bring the slugs and their upwardly mobile cousins, the snails, out in force.

It was not always the case, though. I'm ashamed to admit that there was a time, back in the 1960s, when schoolboys, huddled behind the bike sheds for a playtime fag followed by a mouthful of Polos, considered it highly amusing to stamp on one end of a slug and watch the poor creature's innards shoot out of the other.

Such barbarous behaviour cannot be excused by the fact that we had no pocket computers or mobile phones to occupy us.

But it went on, along with blowing up frogs with straws, shooting birds with airguns and stealing their eggs, burning ants' nests with magnifying glasses, assaulting classmates with spud guns, pea-shooters and laggy bands loaded with ink-soaked blotting paper, cutting worms in half to see if both bits went their separate ways, and jabbing girls' bottoms with compasses in the school dinner queue.

Not like the little horrors of today.

The sex lives of ducks

SPRING is in the air and an old man's thoughts while rambling in the countryside naturally turn to… the love lives of ducks.

I've become something of a twitcher on my regular canalside walks in the Erewash Valley. But enough of my medical problems. I'm here to discuss the bizarre couplings of members of the mallard species, or as we experts call them, *duckus normalus*.

And I can tell you it's like *Tales of the Riverbank* but with an X-certificate.

I've been able to witness their antics close up thanks to the lure of a bag of breadcrumbs and my wife's distinct purple coat. I'm convinced that the ducks occupying a stretch of canal near our home recognise my better half. They certainly talk the same language.

Spring is all about new life and we watch with a warm glow as assorted wildfowl build nests for new arrivals. There are clear signs of care and courtesy among the feathered fraternity.

It all seems so normal. A pair of mallards will head to the canal towpath at first sight of Mrs P's purple coat and the male will hang back while the female feasts.

Imagine a human dad-to-be handing the remains of his kebab to the missus on a night out and you get the picture. But instead of two, Mrs Duck is eating for 12.

Then, one day, we are approached by a female and two males, the nearest of which – hubby, we presume – dutifully holds back as the female has her fill. The other male shows no interest in the food but, at the sight of a FEMALE approaching, springs into action, chasing her through the water and up into the air.

So, who is this gallant third duck, we wonder? A doting grandad-to-be, perhaps, preserving the sanctity of the pairing of a beloved son or daughter as they enjoy a post-wedding feast, fresh from dancing to 'The Birdie Song' at a reception in the bullrushes?

Is he seeing off the advancing female because he knows her type? Perhaps he's spotted her before at the Quackers Hotel, all fishnet stockings and bright red lipstick, clucking 'fancy a little company?' to passing geese. Is he afraid she's out to snare his boy – or his boy's girl?

Then again, his motives might be entirely selfish. He might not be looking out for the young couple at all but biding his time, playing the supportive pal until he can whisk the lady away with fowl intent one night when dad has fallen asleep singing 'Three Little Ducks Went Swimming One Day' to the babies.

Perhaps it's not straightforward duckie nookie on his mind, but a menage á trois.

I can see the tabloid headline now: FEATHERS FLY IN DUCKIE NOOKIE LOVE NEST.

TECHNOLOGY

I've joined the smartphone age

'YOU'RE a typical male!' my wife laughed.

'What do you mean?' I said, wondering if she had in mind 'rugged, dynamic, handsome'.

'You look for things but you can never find them,' she said.

Ah, so that would be 'useless'.

She did have a point. I'd spent five minutes rummaging in a drawer for something I knew I'd put in a safe place. Then she looked in the same place and found it at once.

I resisted the temptation to suggest she'd been hiding it up her sleeve. Life was complicated enough, now that I had a new phone.

After years of loyal service, my trusty old 'brick' was destined for the scrapheap – and I'd only just mastered the art of texting while walking.

It was my 60th birthday and the missus had signed me up for a smartphone, insisting it was high time I joined the 21st century.

So, I charged my new toy and set aside an hour to explore it as I contemplated the task of manually transferring all my contacts, because, this being a surprise gift, the old sim card had been in my possession while Mrs P went birthday shopping.

I have been known to moan about mobile phones killing the art of conversation but I was excited about the prospect of having the internet forever in my hand, though apprehensive at having to learn how to use a new gadget, since that meant thinking seriously about something, a practice I try to avoid these days.

Still, I had the manual to help me. It was entitled *Quick Start Guide*. But as I delved therein, I discovered it was a lesson in deceit that would do a Chancellor proud on Budget Day.

It did not guide me to a start and the only thing it did quickly was tell me to switch the thing on, access the internet and read the user guide online.

This was all too sudden. I wasn't ready for the internet yet. I wanted a helping hand from something crinkly and reliable, like me: an idiot's guide on paper. Instead, I thumbed through 16 pages of 'safety information' with pearls like:

- Do not bite or suck the device or the battery
- Do not insert the device or supplied accessories into the eyes or mouth.

And best of all:

- Do not use the device for anything other than its intended use.

All of which ruled out my plan to use it for facial reconstruction surgery.

But I mustn't grumble, not yet. I've merely dipped a toe into my seventh decade. It will take time to absorb the fact that, by anyone's standards, I'm now an old man, smartphone or not.

Offers of funeral insurance, escorted tours, mobility aids, pension plans, home insulation, orthopaedic beds, easy-grip gardening tools and many more delights – all accompanied by the lure of a free pen or an M&S voucher – will no doubt be pinging my way once the vampires of commerce cotton on to my new status and attempt to bleed me dry.

So there'll be plenty of grist to the grumble mill. And just in case I thought otherwise, the first letter I received as a 60-year-old was to inform me that I'd soon be receiving a little kit so that I could submit a 'sample' for bowel cancer screening.

I hope the quick start guide to that is better than my phone's.

The cashless society

THE prospect of a cashless society comes ever closer with the relentless use of cards and cryptocurrencies.

Fast-forward 20 years. A plump, grey-haired woman stands before a hologram of Wollaton Hall. Fiona Bruce has clearly let herself go.

'Welcome,' she smiles, 'to the *Antiques Roadshow*. And let's see what our visitors have in store for us.'

A silver-haired man in deckchair blazer appears and, beside him, a stooped, wizened me. I have an old wheelbarrow full of bulging carrier bags.

'What on earth do we have here?' says Blazer Man, pulling a handful of metal discs from one of the bags.

'That's pre-decimal coinage, that is,' says I. 'Proper money.'

'Indeed it is!' he laughs. 'How extraordinary. And people used to buy and sell things with this stuff, didn't they? Are you old enough to remember those days?' He winks to camera.

'Sure am,' I give a one-toothed grin. 'This 'un,' I hold up a dark brown metal disc etched with the face of Queen Victoria, 'this were a penny. When I were a kid, you could buy a strip o' toffee for one o' them. Twenty'd buy you a pack o' fags. And if you ever had a pound, well, you were minted! You could get six pints o' mild wi' that and still 'ave enough for t'bus 'ome and a fish 'n' mix.'

There are guffaws from the watching crowd.

'You could indeed,' says Blazer Man. 'There was a vast industry mining the earth's natural resources and producing these, well, erm, rather primitive things in their billions.'

'Aye,' says I, 'and we 'ad tanners and thruppeny bits and florins and half crowns and…'

'Then came the digital age, of course,' says Blazer Man, 'and we got away from sterling and dollars and that sort of thing to what we have now: a secure, eco-friendly, invisible system of currency that whizzes across the world in a nanosecond.'

(Crowd murmurs approval)

'And you've witnessed all of that, ahem, change in your lifetime. Lucky you!'

He takes the penny from my hand and balances it on a tiny set of scales. 'Nine point four grams!' he shrieks. 'And there were 240 of these to that pound you

mentioned. So,' he rubs his chin affectedly, 'that's more than two kilograms in weight.'

(Laughter)

'Goodness, it's a wonder you ever managed a night out if you were carrying that lot around. I do hope you had a strong belt for your trousers! Do you have many of these?'

'Ooh, hundreds,' I beam. 'Some of 'em from 1860. Kept 'em all these years, thinking they might be worth a bob or two one day.'

'Well,' Blazer Man grimaces, 'we do have to talk value and I'm afraid they're not worth much. Nothing at all, in fact. Not even what we'd call a sausage back in the days before meals came in tablet form.

'But,' he smiles, pulling out a penny-sized phone, 'I'll credit you 2.5 noodlebingles for the wheelbarrow.'

Space-age sisters take off

BE prepared to pinch yourself if you're planning to visit a UK airport. You're about to meet the future.

At Birmingham its name is Lucy but other airports will soon be employing her space-age sisters.

They're talking holograms, straight out of a sci-fi movie. They look amazingly like real women, except that they're only a few inches thick (oops, forgot about Kate Moss!). They even speak and move like them: a stunning, if spooky, example of British genius at work.

Costing about £10,000 a time, these digital darlings stand near queues to Security, advising people to get rid of liquids and have their boarding passes ready.

The aim is to cut queues and make life easier for travellers. It's another sign of how our world has been radically transformed by computers.

It won't stop with Lucy and her pals, of course. Before long these virtual beings will be interactive, fitted with buttons so that we can pose questions. And they won't just assist real people, they'll replace them.

Employers will be able to save a fortune by getting rid of receptionists – at libraries, hotels, banks, even doctors' surgeries – and replacing them with holograms that are always polite, don't keep you waiting while they file their nails, don't call in sick with a migraine/hangover and won't – not yet – get pregnant.

One can't help but admire the brilliance of such creations but I do find the growing dehumanisation of modern life slightly disturbing.

Computers have taken much of the grunt out of the world of work. Many of the hard manual jobs that left men and women too worn out or sick to enjoy retirement have been replaced by machines. But it's not all for the better.

We no longer need to meet others to shop or get drunk, because we can buy everything online. People work from home on PCs. Computerised football is so much cosier than getting yourself down the rec with a ball and a few mates. And why venture into the big, bad world when you can make friends on Facebook in the comfort of your little hidey hole?

No wonder that some of the old-fashioned values that guarded us against lawless streets have been eroded. No wonder obesity is rocketing when we barely need lift a finger to eat or be entertained.

Not that I'm against technology. Indeed, if the missus wants to treat me to a pretty, talking hologram to entertain me while she's watching *EastEnders*, I won't object, so long as my virtual friend has something more interesting to say than, 'Place phones and keys in your hand luggage.'

But the gift I'd like more than anything for on my forthcoming birthday is a voice-activated gadget that would shout or beep when I was in close proximity: something to stop me losing all the things I regularly misplace, like car key, wallet, debit card, glasses, work pass – and that thing on top of my shoulders.

Leave my worms alone

WHAT'S 'mmm' my wife asked as we shared an intimate moment.

'Wotchya mean 'what's mmm?' I said.

'I though you said something.'

'Did I?'

This was worrying. So, I suspect, is the vision of me and Mrs P sharing an intimate moment, so let me put your mind at rest: we were using the bathroom at the same time before going to bed. It's one of those things old folk mean when they say marriage is about give and take.

I had been having a conversation with myself while perched on the toilet. It was about something so inconsequential that the sound of my wife's voice immediately knocked it out of my head. I think it had got to the point where I thought 'mmm'. Now, I feared it might have been an audible one.

Had I become one of those old men who can't keep their thoughts to themselves during conversation and are prone to making inappropriate mutterings, loud enough to be heard by sharper ears?

Ah, the joys of being 62 and sliding inexorably into an era increasingly dominated by aches, pains and forgetfulness!

It's bad enough being unable to hear what people say half the time. I'm deaf as a post in one ear because of a condition that might end up requiring minor surgery, while my wife has a long-standing problem with what's medically known as 'me ears', so when I return from work late in the evening and she's semi-asleep on the settee, our conversations go something like this:

She, 'I've done the nnnnn in.'

Me, 'You what?'

She, 'Pardon?'

Me, 'What have you done?'

She, 'The online banking.'

Me, 'Good. Everything OK?'

She, 'What you say?'

Good job we can laugh about it. I wish I could say the same about another irritation in my life, one that can afflict young and old alike.

I'm referring to precious teats, I mean predictive text. It's installed on the email on my tablet and it makes me swear a lot. I'd love to know which crazed nerd came up with such an internal combustion, I mean infernal creation, so that I could tell them I'd spent a lifetime trying to master gramophone and was quite capable of composing my own worms without the aid of a touch-screen forecaster, thank you very mulch.

The machine can't possibly know what I'm trying to write, so why guess? And if it must guess, can't it give me something vaguely sensible?

Local names send it doolally. The Derbyshire village of Spondon, for instance, becomes Swindon, while nearby Breadsall becomes Boardwalk and my beloved Ilkeston turns into Bulletin. If I try to write 'ey up', as one does in my part of the world, it comes out as 'at up'.

It's particularly frustrating when I try to dash off a short email to myself as a reminder for future columns.

For example, I'd read a book about Edward Snowden, the man who leaked thousands of secret files revealing the extent of surveillance by the world's most powerful intelligence agency.

Some of the disclosures mentioned Britain's GCHQ, so I began to write GCHQ on the tablet. But no matter how I tried, the text predictor turned those initials into 'haha'. Honestly!

I eventually tried writing 'gee sea aitch queue' but it came out as 'her see witch queue'.

Do you think someone's watching me? If so, I hope they're having a good laugh.

Driverless cars

ANY doubts I had about renewing my membership of the Machines Are Taking Over the World Society vanished with the government's announcement that driverless cars will soon be allowed on Britain's roads.

Yes, the machine that man invented to move him swiftly from A to B no longer needs him. What next? The pilotless aeroplane? The TV set that watches us?

In the early days of the computerised carriage there'll no doubt be a non-driving passenger or the human variety to keep an eye on things. But it's sure to live up to its name eventually and when it does, men and women who drive for a living will be out of a job and all those who simply enjoy motoring will have to find other pleasures.

There will doubtless be many benefits from this latest example of life imitating science fiction. One of the less obvious could be longer marriages, because researchers in Sweden have found that couples in which one partner commutes for more than 45 minutes per day are 40 per cent more likely to divorce.

Since driverless cars won't have human frailties, there will be fewer crashes, which should mean shorter queues at A&E, except that we'll have to cut the number of doctors and nurses because there'll be fewer people earning money and paying taxes, what with all the cabbies, bus drivers, couriers and truckers thrown out of work.

Traffic cops will become a thing of the past and we won't need as many firefighters and paramedics – or insurance staff, since premiums will be down due to there being fewer claims, which will mean less work for people who run comparison websites and create TV adverts featuring meerkats that spawn a vast industry in soft toy production, so more job losses there.

With less cash from adverts, TV bosses will have less to spend on programmes, so we'll get endless repeats screened to millions more people who are getting fat at home because they have no work to go to.

I'm always one to look on the bright side, however, and humans being the irrational and mischievous souls they are, the driverless car might open new job opportunities.

Imagine: graphic designers could quench the driverless public's thirst for nostalgia by dressing up bog-standard vehicles with a range of retro holograms and tweaking their navigation systems so that they looked and behaved like favourite motors of yesteryear...

Ladies, gentlemen and robots of Future World, I give you:

- The Taxi, guaranteed never to give way to oncoming traffic
- The School Run 4x4, programmed to park on zig-zag lines; and
- The White Van, supplied with virtual dirt in which you can draw your own amusing message (please note, 'I wish my wife was this filthy' comes as standard).

Chips with everything

THE age of the microchipped man has arrived.

Workers in a Swedish office block can now open security doors, operate photocopiers and pay for their lunch in the canteen with a wave of their hand.

It's all thanks to a radio frequency identification chip about the size of a grain of rice. Implanted into the back of the hand, it contains personalised security information that's transmitted to special receivers.

Just imagine where this might lead in five or 50 years.

No more struggling to remember passwords because all you need to access whatever has replaced your PC is your hand.

No trying to hide your PIN at the ATM because who needs cash?

Payday's here and those clever chips that could once only transmit information can now receive it as well, so a handshake with the robot in charge of your workplace or job centre deposits all the what-we-called-cash just below the third knuckle of your left hand.

It's Sunday morning and time for the collection in church. Remember the embarrassment of having just a few coppers in your pocket? Relax! Simply touch the receiver that's replaced the collection plate, enter the amount of your gift and pointlessly try to hide your stinginess from he who sees all.

A quick backhander pays for (driverless) journeys by bus, taxi, plane, ship or train and there's no danger of being stuck at the supermarket checkout with an overloaded trolley and no means to pay because you left home without your what-we-called-cash-card. All you need is your hand.

How about a trip to the what-we-called-a-pub? It's now a shipping container at the end of the street but there are holograms where the bar staff used to be and they're programmed with a nice line in banter to greet you as you select your tipple and place your hand on a receiver that not only deducts the right amount but injects you with a highly concentrated form of said tipple at the optimum rate for taste, comfort and euphoria over a chosen period of time.

But there are perils in this utopian future. The idea was that we alone would have control over what passed between our chip and a receiver. Then the government finds a way of tapping in. Obviously. So, not only can it discover where we are at any moment but it can raid our chip account as and when national fiscal requirements dictate. It might even use the device to transmit a stupefying drug to silence dissenting voices.

Meanwhile, criminals will have taken to stealing chips by any means possible, up to and including amputation.

Back in the real world: I'm being far-fetched and paranoid, of course. After all, no one could force us to wear those chips, could they?

It's up to us if we follow technological trends or not – and we're not sheep, are we? I mean, look at how we nurtured our beloved old ways by resisting one-stop shopping, compact discs, the school run, central heating, TVs in bedrooms, email, dinners on trays, mobile phones, selfies, onesies, Facebook…

FOOD

Love takes Allsorts

A BIT of bread and cheese isn't the obvious ingredient of an act designed to reinvigorate a long and largely happy marriage, so allow me explain.

I consider this combination to be the food of the gods at the right time – towards the end of a holiday full of rich food, perhaps; or, as on the occasion in question, while pushing a heaving trolley around a supermarket and me and the missus salivating in unison at the thought of getting home, tearing open a bag of freshly baked rolls and devouring them with cheese and a cuppa.

And so, while she put away the shopping, I set to work on the butties, asking if she'd prefer her cheese sliced or grated, though I knew she couldn't care less, so sliced it was. As was mine.

That's when her jaw dropped.

Me and sliced cheese had never gone together. Our sons grew to adulthood quoting Dad's insistence on grated cheese in a sandwich as proof that he had ideas above his station.

Now, in a flash, I'd changed, and this didn't merely mean the grater would need washing less frequently in future. The incident had also shown that, after four decades with the same long-suffering woman, I was prepared to take risks to keep our marriage fresh.

I trust she's graterful.

Truth is, I owed her one because she'd stunned me the previous evening at a meeting of the local Mensa society,

I think my wife's gone Bertie.

aka my bunch of old saddos slobbering into their ale in the pub. It was while we were discussing familiar topics such as the shrinking size of Mars bars that my wife made a startling revelation: she habitually deconstructs Liquorice Allsorts.

Now, I knew her favourite Allsort was the thick, cubed variety made up of alternate layers of liquorice and white candy. But not until that moment had I realised that, instead of popping them in whole like any normal person, she peeled them apart and ate them layer by layer.

The news sent a buzz around the increasingly inebriated gathering.

'Haven't had a Liquorice Allsort for ages,' declared one friend.

'Can't beat the ones with hundreds 'n' thousands,' said another.

'Nah,' said a third. 'Those little magic wands are best – as long as you don't get the solid tube of liquorice by mistake. Fancy making them the same shape and si…'

'Never mind that!' I cut in. 'How long' – I cast my beloved an accusing glance – 'has this being going on?'

'Oh, I dunno, ages.'

Casual as you like. As if it meant nothing.

It just goes to show that you can share the same bed with someone nearly all your life and never really know who they are.

But the cheese affair had demonstrated that she's not the only unpredictable one in our marriage and it was in this new spirit of adventure that I decided some days later to buy something for our mutual pleasure. I headed for the pharmacy.

I had hoped I wouldn't have to ask an assistant for help, because I'd probably feel daft, so I spent an age studying the various displays and squinting at the rows of boxes and tubes on shelves behind the counter before stuttering, 'How you got any, erm…'

And at that moment I had a horrible thought: that the young shop assistant was thinking, 'He wants some Viagra but daren't ask. Well, I'm not going to make it easy for him, dirty old devil. He's going to have to come right out with it.'

'…erm, Horlicks tablets,' I said at last, because that's truly what I'd gone in for.

But it transpired that production of that peculiar delicacy had ceased years ago.

Still, I'd tried. And as we enter our fourth decade of marriage, I think Mrs Pheasant and I can be sure of one thing: life will never be boring.

Cricket teas

MUCH as I enjoy the summer, it's a dangerous time for me because I spend much of it watching cricket.

'Ah, no wonder,' the philistines among you are thinking, 'the poor thing must be out of his mind.'

Listen: you stick to truly boring sports, like golf and motor racing, and leave the good stuff to the rest of us, OK?

I've been a cricket fan since I could pick up a ball and, besides, I'm hanging on as proprietor of Dad's Taxi for as long as elder son can bear the embarrassment of me following his performance in the sport of gentlemen.

But to the perils: they come not from driving to back-of-beyond grounds served by potholed tracks; not even from my role as a part-time umpire, though the latter is laced with danger – the ball hammered straight back down the pitch, sending me squirming for safety with a blast of ungentlemanly language, for instance; the sun beating down on my bald bits; the unspoken threats of retribution from the batsmen who's just getting his eye in when my trigger finger sends him back to the pavilion, out LBW.

No, the real danger comes from food.

Umpires qualify for tea with the players, you see, and cricket teas have one wonderful thing in common: they're all buffets. It's down to the home side to provide tea at the interval and, with 60 quid or so at their disposal from the players' subs, the wives, aunts, sisters and grannies roped in to do this task can create some miraculous – or meagre – spreads.

One of my all-time favourites was in the north Derbyshire village of Clowne, where homemade scones with fresh strawberries were on offer. But even a bottom-of-the-league buffet is a thing of beauty because it's so easy to put away those dinky little sausage rolls, egg mayo sarnies, quiches, pizza slices and jam tarts. They vanish almost before I can say 'owzat' and fill another plate.

And because cricket takes up at least half a day, I never have time for a proper meal – something with vegetables – at weekends, so my diet consists largely of stodge, and with each passing summer, my health deteriorates as my waistline expands.

It's a hard life, isn't it?

I can't wait for younger son's football season to start. At least his games are soon over and the only food temptation comes from a hotdog van run by a chain-smoking man with grubby fingernails.

Save me from fruity cheese

IF flushing loos are one benchmark of civilisation, easy access to one's favourite cheese is surely another, which is why I've fallen out with Tesco.

Before anyone brands me an Asda agent in disguise, let to me say that I'm a Tesco devotee, not at all surprised by the company's phenomenal success. But it does have some annoying tricks, one of which is to reel us in with new products, then whip them away.

I'd just about got into the habit of buying a particular brand of cholesterol-reducing milk (too little, too late, obviously) when it disappeared from the shelves. My real beef, however, is about white Stilton, my favourite cheese since childhood.

My wife and kids aren't keen on what they call 'banana cheese', so I'd pick up only a small pack during our weekly shop. And then it vanished from the Tesco shelves, without a word of apology or explanation.

Never mind, I thought at first, it's just a blip. But the weeks turned into months and as I scoured the shelves in vain, I was taunted by the thoroughbred's banjo-twanging cousins: blue Stilton, white Stilton with cranberries, white Stilton with apricots, white Stilton with mango and ginger – but no pure white Stilton as the cheese god intended it.

During all this frantic searching, my cholesterol was reaching dangerously low levels and I began to think that perhaps Tesco's customer profiling was so accurate that it was all a plot to improve my diet.

As is often the case, though, truth is stranger than fiction and the truth, according to a girl on the deli counter, is that Tesco splits stores into different zones for product supply and my home town of Ilkeston is not in the zone for white Stilton, though nearby Heanor is.

Armed with this information, I headed for the customer relations desk to file a complaint. There I found a member of staff of more mature years, and very polite and attentive she was, while probably thinking 'get a life, you sad old nutter'. I now await a reply from head office with bated breath uncontaminated by Parfum de Stilton.

Meanwhile I'd love to know who's getting paid to decide that the inhabitants of one former mining town are more likely than those of another just four miles away to like bits of fruit in their cheese.

Sugar has addled my brain

LAZING after a large family meal, my grown-up sons sprawled on the sofa, a spoon apiece, and devoured leftover pudding from a single, messy plate with childish glee. They might just as well have been mmm-ing their way through something fancy in a posh restaurant, but it was merely a mess of caramel-flavoured ice cream, raspberry jelly and strawberry Angel Delight.

You can't beat cheap puddings. Think jam roll and custard. Or sliced bananas and custard. Or custard.

It struck me that I'd been eating Angel Delight for 50 years, though not continuously.

I'd been reading a newspaper article marking 50 years since the Summer of Love. I knew 1967 was a time of huge cultural, scientific and political change, when hippies got high and skirts even higher, putting far too much female flesh on show than was good for prepubescent boys like me.

But I hadn't realised it was the year in which Angel Delight first appeared, though I clearly remember it muscling out Instant Whip as a quick-pud favourite in the Pheasant household. The Whip had been on the scene for years but took a lot of arm ache to whisk into mousse-like form, while the Angel was ready in a few minutes, and sweeter.

My powers of recall were in for a battering, though, when I looked up other 1967 food inventions on the internet.

Fab ice-lollies seemed spot-on 1967, and indeed that's when they first appeared. I can't recall the world of 'suckers' before Fab arrived with his red-ice trousers, creamy white tunic and chocolate waistcoat decked with rainbow sprinkles, but I know life was never quite the same again.

But Twix, supreme master of the biscuit-caramel-chocolate combo? I'm convinced I didn't discover Twix until I was in my 20s, which would be 1974 onwards.

How wrong I was.

Then along came an Angel.

Twix, I discovered, first went on sale in 1967, which meant I lost at least seven years of Twix-eating that I'll never get back.

More unsettling news was to come from my internet trawl of choccie nostalgia.

I distinctly remember when Aztec bars appeared. This Cadbury creation of nougatine, caramel and chocolate went head to head for children's affections with the mighty Mars and was a halfpenny cheaper. The TV ads were filmed inside a real Aztec temple and cardboard cutouts of Aztec warriors appeared in supermarkets.

I checked Cadbury's website and gasped as I discovered that Aztec bars first went on sale in 1967. This threw me completely, because I had a friend at junior school who always had more tuck money than the rest of us and I could have sworn that every day on our way to school, when we called at a dusty little sweet shop run by a bewhiskered old lady and I bought my Milky Way, he would splash out on an Aztec.

But we left that school in 1965, two years before Aztec bars were invented.

How could my memory be so far out of kilter? Perhaps I did too much sherbet in the '60s

I was discussing this with an old friend when he put my anguish in context. Growing up, he recalled, he and his brother had to share virtually everything – but then came 1967 and my friend got his first job.

'And that,' he said wistfully, 'was the first time I ever had a whole bar of chocolate to myself.'

Lettuce pray

'WOULD you like some lettuce?' It was a perfectly reasonable question, given that I had half a one going off in the fridge, but it was 11am on a Sunday and my son's girlfriend was curled up on the sofa with a coffee.

'What is *wrong* with you?' she giggled. 'Why are you asking me that?'

'I meant for your rabbits,' I said, but she now thought more than ever that I was weird.

The really odd thing about this exchange is that it put 'like' and 'lettuce' in the same sentence.

Lettuce be honest: there's nothing much to like about the stuff. Nothing much to dislike either. It just *is*.

Wet, crunchy at times, green, one of five a day and good for you, which is why I slip it between other salad items in a sandwich – tasty things like tomato, avocado, beetroot, pepper (but never, ever ghastly cucumber!). But taste-wise: zero. And it gets in the way of a good dollop of mayo.

'Rich in essential nutrients' it may well be; full of half the alphabet in vitamins, perhaps. But where's the joy? Where the dancing tastebuds? If someone served me a mixed salad with dandelion leaves in place of lettuce, I doubt I'd notice.

It's such a faff as well. All that slicing and chopping, then washing between the folds in case something – probably tastier and more nutritious – lurks within.

Or you buy a bag of it, ready to eat, and after using less than half, fold it up and stuff it under something heavier in the bottom of the fridge, where it's gone brown and slimy by the time you next want some, so you throw it away – and we Brits do so in vast quantities. Forty per cent of bagged salad is binned, apparently, amounting to 37,000 tonnes of food waste per year

And once you've eaten some, there's sure to be a sliver stuck between your teeth, defying all efforts to work it free with a finger end.

The health benefits seem undeniable. Eating lettuce regularly is said to guard against osteoporosis, heart disease and dementia.

You can't knock the lettuce PR machine but it's yet to convince me that there's something to 'like'.

I'm surprised no one has spotted a gap in the market and produced a foodstuff that combines all the goodness of lettuce with something that tastes great – the sort of thing that would make me jump out of bed in a morning, shouting, 'I want lettuce!'

Perhaps they should make a highly concentrated form of lettuce and pack it into a tiny chocolate-flavoured biscuit. Now wouldn't that be a little gem?

Hidden peril in cakes

COMETH the cake, cometh the man. And so to Canvey Island, in Essex, where one school made headlines and had 'elf n safety' critics in raptures by banning triangular flapjacks because a boy was hit in the face by one.

Perhaps, like me, you think that unruly behaviour is the real issue here. Perhaps you, too, are puzzled by the school's decision to serve only square or rectangular flapjacks in future, as if they couldn't cause injury when flung with force by some little horror in the school canteen.

Have they no ingenuity? Why not round flapjacks? Or flapjacks with spongy edges?

I bet the good folk at the Health and Safety Executive sighed with relief that it was nothing to do with them. They've endured years of ridicule over some of the daft things done in their name – hanging baskets banned in case someone bumps their head; school kids told to wear clip-on ties; candy floss on sticks outlawed in case people trip and impale themselves… that sort of thing.

As an HSE spokesman said of the flapjack farce, 'We often come across half-baked decisions taken in the name of health and safety, but this one takes the biscuit.'

Boom, boom!

Behind most silly stories, however, is a serious point and this one is no different: cakes can indeed be dangerous.

A stripper in Italy died while waiting in a giant cake to surprise the groom at his stag party. In Wales, a man choked to death in a fairy cake-eating contest.

And even in normal circumstances there may be peril in a pastry. The jam tart, for instance, is a picture of innocence but the slightest tear of its tinfoil case while extricating said tart can inflict a nasty finger wound.

The cup cake is more brazen. Little silver balls sprinkled on top look great but can cause dental havoc.

You and I know an Eccles cake when we see one but who's to say a small child might not pick up a lump of fly infested dough by mistake?

An elephant's foot is delightful when eaten with decorum but biting roughly into its tarpaulin of a pastry case might unleash a jet of cream fit to take an eye out.

Even grandma's favourite, the baked egg custard, is a devil in disguise. If the brown skin on top is too rubbery to break with first bite, it may become stuck fast over mouth and nostrils, resulting in a condition known as nutmeg brain.

I think they caught something like that in Essex.

My *MasterChef* moment

NOW come on: there's no way amateur cooks can rustle up some of the dishes we see on TV's *MasterChef* in the allotted time without some behind-the-scenes help. Or a toy clock.

On one recent show, a contestant allegedly produced a bread basket filled with lamb and barley stew; battered chilis stuffed with spiced potato; a cucumber raita; and a lime-water drink – in NINETY minutes. It takes me that long to write a shopping list.

If John Torrode and Gregg Wallace want to see reality cooking in action, they should come to my house when I'm preparing my pack-up for work.

John, 'What are you making for us today, Pete?'

Me, 'It's one of my favourites, John – Scandinavian salad wrap with lime and chilli chicken.'

John, 'And for dessert?'

Me, 'Chocolate and caramel surprise.'

Gregg, 'Sounds simple but could be delicious. You've got half an hour. Off you go!'

Ten minutes gone: I've filled the area between kettle and bread bin with a plastic tub of tomatoes, a bag of chopped lettuce, a lump of Cheddar in clingfilm, an avocado and a jar of spicy mayo

'Pete, Pete, Pete!' wails Gregg. 'Why are working on the smallest space in the kitchen when you've a large working surface next to you?'

'It's tradition,' I say, flustered, as I reach for the freezer door and pull out a pack of tortillas and a bag of lime and chilli pieces.

Off-camera, 'Ah, the Scandinavian element,' Gregg laughs. 'He's bought that chicken from Iceland! Pete's got all the ingredients for a classic wrap. Now, all he's got to do is put them together.'

'But what's he showing us about his cooking skills?' says John.

'I know what you mean,' says Gregg. 'He's using a microwave for his tortilla and his chicken. But, John, he's got to defrost them perfectly! Too little and that chicken will be inedible. Too much and that tortilla will be like wet paper. Then he's got to get them to that cramped worktop without dropping them.'

'I think he's got his hands full,' says John.

Twenty minutes gone: the tortilla is covered with shreds of lettuce and sliced tomato.

'Ten minutes left,' says John. 'How are you for time?'

'Fine, I think. Just got to lay the chicken pieces on top, slice the avocado, add some cheese and give it a squirt of mayo.'

Gregg says quietly, 'Pete's put that tub of tomatoes and bag of lettuce back in the fridge beautifully. He's cut the top off that avocado without bloodshed AND he's now covering his filling with cheese that he's grated himself.

'He's used a squeezy bottle to pipe the mayo over his filling and now he's folding the corner of that tortilla over and rolling it forward into a yummy tube of food that he's going to slice in half at an angle. He's shown us some real technical skills today.'

'Time's up!'

I cheat just long enough to enclose the two pieces in tinfoil.

'I'm impressed,' says John. 'But where's your dessert?'

I reach into a cupboard and pull out two Twix bars. 'Cracking!' says Gregg.

BLOKES AND CLOTHES

Who put those man boobs there?

I'M standing at the bar of our local when my mate says, 'I like your jacket, is it new?'

'Yeah,' say I. 'Is yours?'

'Yeah,' he beams 'So's the shirt and the jeans.'

Rewind a few hours…

I'm replenishing my wardrobe as a pre-Christmas present to myself.

Clothes and I have a strange relationship; I'm hard to please but once I've found something I like, I wear it to death. Result: entire outfits look faded and tatty.

There was a time, in my 40s, when I dreaded looking like mutton dressed as lamb. These days I think sod it. I'm not yet ready to be a mannequin in Marks and Sparks' older-man range. And I'm too old for rips and pins and backsides hanging out.

So, I'm in Next, which has become the Burton's of my youth, in that it's close to home, not too expensive and has a reasonable range of clothes – a bit bland but not down-wid-de-kids.

My wife waits patiently as I pile up a selection of garments and head for the changing rooms. I swear that 20 minutes in one of those tiny cubicles is more exhausting than a 20-minute run.

Hangers bend and twang and fall to the floor as I grow ever more exasperated and sweaty while trying to release them from buttoned-up jeans and shirts. All that over-the-head activity makes the tufts of grey and black that pass for my hair these days stick up like devil horns.

The quest for jeans that fit both leg and waist seems destined for defeat until the day I die.

Urgh! I just caught sight of my naked chest in the mirror.

I try on a sweatshirt with half a T-shirt sewn inside. It looked good on the display rail but someone's slipped a pair of man boobs inside it.

I settle on a conventional shirt with lumberjack pattern and try not to think it's like something my mother bought for me from a market stall when I was a lad.

It's actually not bad – but what's this infernal button arrangement? I've only just got used to a denim shirt with press studs from last Christmas. Putting that one on requires an honours degree in hand-to-eye co-ordination but at least it's beautifully simple to rip off last thing at night, unlike the infernal hybrid I'm now wrestling with: buttons from neck to belly, then press studs down the rest of the front and on the cuffs.

It's a madness test for fools.

I envisage myself home from the pub tonight, trying to unbutton the studs and sending buttons pinging around the bedroom.

Finally, energy and patience exhausted, I head for home, knowing that I've staved off the tramp in me for a few more months.

So, me and my middle-aged mate are standing at the bar, discussing clothes like they're the new rock 'n' roll and the landlady's giggling and saying we're like a pair of girls.

All of which I could cope with, but my new jacket has one final indignity. It's pleather, as in plastic, with two faux metal buttons on each cuff, and every time I move, they jingle.

How very appropriate at this time of year: I've turned into Rudolph the ruddy reindeer.

The wonder of shoelaces

YOU wouldn't think that shoelaces could be a source of endless fascination, would you? Bear with me as I recall a voyage that began with a trip to buy some shoes for work.

I knew exactly what I wanted but, as I trailed around city centre shops, the closest I came was when I spotted a single shoe somewhere on a display, somewhere in a shop, somewhere in the city centre. It was a touch out of my price range, so on I went to four or five more stores before deciding that the single shoe (assuming it had a partner) was for me, and retraced my steps... but couldn't find it anywhere.

It was like some twisted version of Cinderella.

I did finally settle on a pair, with only two drawbacks: the laces were stiff like parcel string and they were done up in what's officially termed the 'shoe shop technique' – that is, one end goes from bottom eyelet on one side to top eyelet on the other, while the other end goes diagonally to the next eyelet up on the other side, then straight across, and so on.

This method annoys me. I can never pull tight enough on the laces to give my shoes a close fit. Still, it wasn't a deal breaker: I'd just have to buy some new laces and tie them the way I'd done since childhood – the straightforward criss-cross technique.

There's little wonder that grumpy old men get even grumpier when specialist shoes shops don't sell spare laces. But I have learnt to breathe and relax. And a few days later, my wife was passing a cobbler's and bought a traditional black pair, happy that they'd be the perfect length because she'd told the shopkeeper how many eyelets were involved.

Oh, how I laughed when they turned out to be way too long, leaving me with the choice of cutting them shorter and causing unsightly frayed ends, or tying them in a double bow. I chose the latter and have regretted it ever since because when I come to take my shoes off at the end of a long day, the laces have managed to tie themselves in knots.

If all this has left you wondering how someone can get so wound up over shoelaces, you should go on the internet and key 'tying shoelaces' into a search engine. You'll find an incredible website created by a 53-year-old Australian called Ian Fieggen, nicknamed Professor Shoelace.

YouTube tutorial by 'Prof Shoelace' Ian Fieggen.

He not only lists 46 ways to lace shoes but explains them with step-by-step graphics, accompanied by photos and even videos. Among them is what he calls CIA Lacing – apparently, a set of methods used by American agents in the Cold War as a form of covert signalling.

The site includes a shoelace length calculator, shoelace tips, frequently asked questions (example, 'Why are my shoelace bows crooked?') and links to other shoelace websites, of which there are many.

There's even Shoelace News, featuring dozens of true stories from around the world, including those of a man killed when his shoelace got caught in a grain auger; a doctor who delivered a baby on a plane, using shoelaces to clamp the umbilical cord; a woman who sued the local council after falling on her face when her lace got caught on a park bench; and a couple, who first met when he saw her in a cinema and tied one of her plaits to her seat with his lace.

Professor Shoelace, I salute you. You've made me feel quite normal.

A right titfer

'GET yourself a hat,' my family nag as we prepare for a holiday in Portugal. 'You'll need one. Especially now, what with…'

'Yeah, I get the picture,' I huff, 'now that I've not got much hair, you mean? OK, hardly any. And if I don't get a hat I'll end up looking more like Fried Tuck than Friar Tuck.'

So off I go hat shopping. Call me girlie but I don't mind shopping; I quite like it, in fact – as long as it's for food, furniture, or electrical gadgets. But not for clothes and especially not for hats.

I've never been a hat person, not since schooldays, when I alternated between a balaclava to keep out the snowballs, and a school cap that I turned into a serious weapon, thrown Oddjob-style from James Bond.

Then I spent a few years with long hair – shoulder-length, though my kids can scarcely believe it – and no hat was going to ruffle my flowing locks.

I don't mind a hood but I guess a parka or duffel coat wouldn't quite cut it on the beach at Albufeira.

But I know a hat makes sense in the sun. It's just a case of finding the one that looks the least ridiculous. Trouble is, every time I try one on and look in a shop mirror, I break out in a sweat. Not sure if this is from anxiety or the extra layer but it doesn't help.

I've begun to wonder if I simply don't have a very hat-friendly head. Perhaps my shape's the runt of the litter in the hat designers' store of head models, the one they only use if there's an odd bit of material left.

This feeling grows as I flit from department store to sports shop, passing numerous men of similar age who look, if not resplendent, then at least at home in their varied headgear. One, knocking 70, manages to pull off an orange and white bandana. Mind you he does have an earring.

Stop being so damned vain, I tell myself. It's just something to keep the sun out – and besides, who's going to care what you look like on holiday, thousands of miles from anyone you know and who'd probably post a picture on Facebook? Ah, wait a minute: our grown-up sons are going with us.

I end up back at the first department store and seek out the uninspiring selection of hats next to the racks of gloves and wallets.

First to face the mirror is a baseball cap, maroon with three meaningless initials on an enormous stiff peak: too yoof. Next, a flat cap: too pigeon fancier. Then a Panama: too diplomat. A sun hat: too cricket umpire. A bucket hat: too Bill and Ben.

Finally, a pork pie hat. Now I know why hats are called titfers. But it's the least hideous, so I bite the bullet and head home, hoping for approval from the better half.

'Could you perhaps do with a larger size?' she asks gently.

'That's the biggest one there was!' I snap. 'Huh. I won't wear it then.'

She tries to make amends later, by which time I've been softened up by both sons and their partners greeting my new look with dropped eyes, pursed lips and shaking shoulders.

'It does look nice, really,' says Mrs P. 'It's probably just that you've had your hair cut and your ears look bigger.'

Oh, thanks very much!

MANWATCHING

March of the NIMs

OF all the irritating people who cross my path – and the older I get, the more numerous they become – none irk me more than NIMs.

NIM stands for No Incoming Messages and denotes a peculiar breed whose communication equipment is permanently set at transmit-only.

The NIM is closely related to the MEME, who talk only about themselves, though MEMEs at least appear to receive incoming conversation before turning it back to themselves.

I came across a thoroughbred NIM leaning against the bar when I popped in to an unfamiliar pub.

He sucked me in with a welcoming pleasantry – 'nice evening, mate' – before unleashing his transmission.

NIM, 'I've just come back from Eye Beetsa, mate. Lovely, it was. Ever been?'

ME, 'No, I haven't. I've visited some of the other Spanish…'

NIM, 'Aye. You can't beat Eye Beetsa. Food's grand, and cheap, and the beaches – out of this world.'

ME, 'As good as Greece?'

NIM, 'Never been, mate – but not a patch on Eye Beetsa.'

And on he droned, with not the slightest interest in what I had to say, just the sound of his own vacuous voice, and I was thinking: why doesn't he find a deserted shed or a field in the middle of nowhere and bore himself witless? Or the fast lane of a motorway.

Most politicians are NIMs but have perfected the art of appearing to listen before reverting to type.

NIMS are the same people who see you loading your car at a supermarket and wait for your space to become available, no matter how long it takes and without a care for the tailbacks they're causing, simply so that they have five yards less to walk.

NIMS pass through shop doors you've kindly held open for them, without a word of acknowledgement.

Bitter experience has finally taught me to pull the plug on them and walk away at the first hint of someone set to transmit only, which is rather sad, because striking up conversation with strangers is a great way to make new friendships.

NIMs don't see it that way. They think all they have to do is talk and the whole world will be enchanted.

I wonder, in the odd generous moment, whether they weren't born with the right equipment. Perhaps they were never listened to as children. Or perhaps, as folk say round my way, they're just pig ignorant.

There may well be a scientific explanation, though. A favourite comic of my youth portrayed tiny creatures inside a man's head, pulling the strings behind every word and deed. Picture the scene in a NIM's brain:

CHIEF BRAIN OPERTOR, 'Anything to report, Mr Pleb?'

PLEB BRAIN OPERATOR, 'Our man's talking to a stranger, chief. Sounds like he might have something interesting to sa…'

CHIEF BRAIN OPERATOR, 'Very good! Ever heard of Eye Beetsa, Mr Pleb?'

Women of the wild

GRAPPLING with wild beasts and braving killer fumes: it sounds like a Saturday night on the pull in some of the less salubrious nightspots in my home town.

In fact, these are vivid memories of the brilliant television series *Human Planet*, which I caught up with recently.

Amateur anthropologists like me, with only beer tickets for a budget, can't hope to top David Attenborough's portrayal of man's struggles with nature.

But a nighttime foray into the wilds of my home town proved that the wonders of mankind are never far away.

In a remote region known as the Three Horsehoes, I encountered two striking specimens of the female form: *deafus apost* and *gobus maximus*.

The natives in this ancient watering-hole were enjoying a tribal custom called 'the turn' – a solo guitarist doing Pink Floyd covers – but it was when my group ventured outside into the less hospitable climes of the smoking shelter that I made my first sighting.

As on all the best safaris, it happened when least expected. An ageing specimen emerged from the gloom, face like thunder.

'Damned noise!' she shrilled, head jerking pubwards. 'Goes right through you. Ridiculous having it that loud.'

I smiled warily.

'Even worse when you've got hearing aids. I've got two and it drives you mad.'

'Turn them off then,' my mate suggested.

''Snot the point,' she snarled. 'Just no need to have it that loud.'

We ummed and nodded, hoping she might retreat to a safe distance.

'Do you lot often come here when they have bands on?'

'Yeah, it's good,' my friend said.

'Well,' she huffed, 'I just hope they've got a good supply of hearing aids when you get older.'

'So do I,' said my wife. 'I've got tinnitus already.'

'Me too,' said the creature. 'It's even worse when you've got tittinus.'

Back inside, I confronted the missus, 'I didn't know you'd got tinnitus.'

'I haven't,' she smiled. 'I was just saying that to wind her up.'

Our conversation was soon lost in the noise of another strange creature in full flow, this one younger and more colourful.

I'd been vaguely aware of her perched on a stool a few yards away. Then came a sound that made my jaw drop: a torrent of shrieks masquerading as aimless conversation with a nearby male, evidently its mate.

I froze in mid-sentence, as if someone had torn out my cerebral cortex and twanged it like an elastic band.

I dared to face her. Was it really a woman, or a giant macaw in fancy dress?

I felt sorry for her mate. Whatever feminine charms she might possess, the poor man was condemned to that racket day and night. I remembered those African hunters in *Human Planet* who strode into a lions' den and stole a haunch of wildebeest. In contrast, to my shame, I lacked the courage to reach out to this woman's partner in gentle conversation.

But if he happens to read this and fancies a holiday with a difference, I can recommend the Borneo jungle.

There he might find the Great Malay Argus, a six-foot-long member of the pheasant family (no relation), which boasts a spectacular mating ritual. It also has one of the loudest voices in the bird world, but I suspect his girlfriend could give it a run for its money.

The Empty Wheelchair

THERE'S an old man in my neighbourhood who takes his disabled wife everywhere in her wheelchair, except that she's dead.

He can be seen in the same town centre pub at the same time on the same day of each week, pushing an empty wheelchair the mile or so from home and back, occasionally calling for a bag of chips to share with his beloved.

It's some months, to my knowledge, since his wife died.

How sad, you might think, as did I at first. But the more I see him, the more I realise that he's happy in his odd way, clinging to shreds of comfort in the twilight of his days, oblivious to the stares of passersby.

I wonder if he has children. Do they know of his eccentricity? Have they tried to persuade him to let go of that bittersweet relic of his marriage and start to build afresh?

I'd like to think that if ever I was so struck by heartache that I lost my grip on reality, my kids would sit me down and give me a good talking-to.

And yet I find the fact that this old man is still out there strangely comforting as life's egg timer grows ever more bottom-heavy and I ponder a future without dependent children or work to occupy me.

Odd characters like him show there's more to growing old than vegetating in a nursing home alongside other frail and confused souls – many of them put there, I'm sure, with the best of intentions by sons and daughters too caught up in the whirl of modern life to have an elderly relative about the house.

Today's children are spoilt in many ways but most are deprived of an experience enjoyed by many of my generation: that of sharing the family home with a widowed grannie whose life revolved around making the gravy for Sunday dinner, then falling into a toothless, windy snooze in front of the telly, stirring in time to sing along to *The Black and White Minstrel Show*, with a Woodbine in one hand and a glass of stout in the other.

But of all the thoughts stirred by that old man and his ghostly wife, the one that lingers is this: somewhere out there, perhaps not far from him, there'll be a lonely, arthritic old lady who'd jump at the chance, if only she could, of meeting a friend with an empty wheelchair.

Homo Halfwitticus and the litter beasts

WHO can have failed to notice a modern-day plague on our countryside?

I refer to the strange creatures let loose on roadside verges with no thought for indigenous wildlife in the fields and woods beyond. So serious is the threat to established fauna and flora should these mutants progress to our fields and woodlands that I embarked on a fact-finding safari.

Beside a busy stretch of road on the Derbyshire-Nottinghamshire border, I found an astonishing number and variety of animals of the genus Dumpus Litteritis, discarded and bewildered.

Here, the lesser dappled Fantabottle with its orange and blue markings; there, a lonely Hula Hoopapotamus, resplendent in red and cream.

Nearby lay the lifeless form of Cannus Carlingus, crushed beneath mighty wheels. Yards away, a fine Cocadoodledo reached for a world beyond the hedgerows, a world free of exhaust fumes. But for one Pepsimax Piglet the dream was over. The poor thing lay flattened and forlorn and one could only imagine the grief of its multipack family.

Cast away, some distance back from the tarmac, a giant of the litter-beast invasion still bore its birth-tag: Lec – the only clue to its former role in domestic refrigeration. Among clumps of grass and nettles nearby, a Banded Bago'fries, a Bigmaccosaurus and several Strawsnakes had escaped their crumpled brown-paper home, whose golden arch plumage was barely visible.

Saddest of all was an upturned Trolleyadour, its wire coat gleaming in the July sun. Having fled the wilds of Asdaland, it had become grounded in a brave attempt to cross a stream.

Imagine, dear reader, what would happen if such creatures were given free rein to roam this green and pleasant land. And yet it is not their fault. They have not chosen to be where they are. Most would have dreamt of a final resting-place in the Great Litter Bin in the Sky.

Braver souls than I have traced the source of this menace back to the human jungle of a nearby town centre, where a sub-species known as Homo Halfwitticus gathers at feeding spots called Kayeffsea and Maccidees.

Some of this breed have been spotted halting their vehicles at the roadside and hurling litter beasts on to grass verges. On being hailed from a safe distance, they will gesture angrily and grunt in their native tongue.

Though difficult to interpret precisely, the message is clear, 'What the ****'s it got to do with you, you interfering old ****? S'only bittta litter, innit? Not 'urt nobody, that not. S'all bi-degra wotsit anyroad.'

And, on being asked what about the vermin their activities might attract, they'll reply, 'Not my concern, innit? Wot you fink I pay mi council tax for?'

You can't beat a good queue

I HAD hoped to discover a special term for a plague that has been visited upon civilised society but, having scoured the internet, the best I can find is 'retractable rope barrier'.

RRBs I'll call them, because we all like a good set of initials.

You must know the sort of thing: metal or plastic poles, about a metre high, set on circular bases, joined by lengths of stretchy fabric and arranged in rows to make sure that customers don't all try rushing to the front at once but snake their way along in serried, shuffling ranks like the good little sheep they are.

They're everywhere, from banks and building societies to concert venues and airports.

Whoever came up with the idea of making people walk umpteen times across the width of a building to reach a point a fraction of that distance from where they joined a queue has spawned a lucrative business for RRB manufacturers and suppliers. Once it became generally accepted that crowd control was needed to save post office clerks from hordes of grannies fighting to be first to buy second-class stamps, it was simply a case of: cue, a business opportunity.

And so the citizen is made to suffer for trying to get their hands on what is rightfully theirs as quickly as possible. Such suffering on a grand scale was in evidence as I flew home from holiday in Spain.

Arriving at East Midlands Airport is never the best way to sustain the holiday spirit and it was about to get worse. After a bendy-bus ride across the tarmac and a 50-yard walk through an extended bus shelter, past a dismal back yard and a 'welcome' mural decorated with potted plants, the doors opened on an arrivals hall packed with what was clearly more than one plane-load of travellers.

Between me and the passport desks looped eight or more rows of RRBs, filled with so many people that my group was guided into a side room – to follow another elasticated snake. When we finally emerged, we were near the front of the main group and then had to walk to the back of it to take our places… a few yards from where we'd come in.

From touchdown to clearing Passport Control took 40 minutes. I could have tolerated this if I was about to reach the Promised Land and was waiting in a queue marshalled by angels, but not two fresh-faced teenagers and a car park attendant in hi-vis jackets.

The urge to break free of the tyranny of the RRB grows whenever I see one. I picture myself ducking under or striding over one. Then I remember my dodgy back and wonder if I might do myself a mischief down below. There's only one thing for it, I'm afraid: get in line.

CHRISTMAS

A conference of Santas

IN the unlikely event that you are a child of impressionable age, please look away. I'm about to explode a Santa Claus myth.

There is more than one Father Christmas.

I'm sorry but that's the truth.

And if you'd already suspected that one portly chap with a white beard and a few reindeer couldn't possibly cover the entire globe in one night, confirmation comes from what has been dubbed St Nickileaks – the publication by internet whistleblower Edward Snowball of thousands of emails sent between discontented elves.

These reveal that, in keeping with the 12 Days of Christmas, there are 12 Santas, each representing a different part of the world, each having equal rank and powers.

The leaked correspondence shows that all 12 red-robed gentlemen (the question of LBGTQ+ membership is still to be settled) along with reindeer representatives, attended the 2016 Santa Conference, held in a giant stocking suspended from the ice-covered surface of Lapland.

Topics discussed included:

- Dismay at the number of parents putting out glasses of Prosecco for Father Christmas on the big night. 'Give me a decent vodka or at least a sweet sherry!' said Russian Santa. 'All that gas is enough to blow one off course.'

- Carrot batons being left out 'for Rudolph'. African Prancer told the conference that other reindeer were fed up of Rudolph getting all the glory, as if he could haul Santa and his cargo across the skies single-hoofedly. But, more importantly, Prancer said, neatly sliced and scrubbed batons were no good at all for reindeer, who preferred them as nature intended, complete with tops and a bit of muck.

- Problems caused by increased home security. Being invisible on Christmas Eve, Santa is not troubled by CCTV but the growing use of alarm systems means elves are having to spend more time on the code for Santa's magic key, which, as all children know, is how he gets in when chimney access is not available.

- Elf and safety. Delegates were disturbed to note an increase in cases of repetitive strain injury among elves constantly testing video games.
- A rise in Santa obesity levels linked to householders who've abandoned traditional mince pies in favour of the new-fangled icing-topped variety.
- Red tape. There was far too much of it, the conference agreed. Clear Sellotape was much better.

The issue that most excited delegates, though, was the need for training to address a skills imbalance among Santa's helpers. Some elves, the conference heard, were proficient at cutting out jigsaw puzzles and making Mr Potato Heads but hopeless at crafting smartphones.

'Children expect so many fancy gifts these days,' said Chinese Santa, 'that my elves can ho-ho-honly just cope.'

The joys of Christmas shopping

CHRISTMAS shopping: two words that strike dread in the heart, though I've never felt as strongly about it as the man who threw himself off a fifth-floor balcony in China because his girlfriend insisted on visiting yet another clothes store.

This year, the curtain rises on my production of *A Nightmare On High Street* during a week off work, designed to recharge my batteries ahead of the ritual extravagance. After three days of decorating, it's almost a comic treat but I soon discover there is plenty to nourish the festive grinch.

Scene 1: Wife tries on shoes in M&S. Old biddy sidles up to her and witters on about how Clark's shoes are so much better, especially if you've got wide feet and ask for children's sizes. We silence her with two servings of cold shoulder.

Scene 2: Everything in this clothes shop is retro/vintage! It's as if the contents of my late-70s wardrobe has been brought back to life, but I can't wear it now without looking like an imposter.

Scene 3: Been shopping for at least an hour, so it's time to eat. Find a café that doesn't begin with 'Star' or end in 'Nero' and refuse to be cowed by sallow-faced street drinkers lolling about in doorway. Watch from inside as police arrive to move them on. Over soup, wife devises political manifesto for dealing with layabouts, key policies being food vouchers instead of cash that they'd only spend on Special Brew, and public flogging for jeans worn halfway down the backside. She's getting worse than me.

Scene 4: Scour ladieswear section of department store for something, anything, to make Mrs P's eyes light up. 'It smells of old women in here. Or is it me?' she whispers. 'I'm used to it,' I laugh.

Scene 5: Wife hangs nose over yet another pair of unsuitable shoes. 'Would you like to try them on?' asks young assistant and laughs as wife replies, 'Only if you can take six inches off the heels.'

Scene 6: Toilet stop, whereupon my innermost secrets are laid bare by toilet roll dispenser that creaks loudly with every sheet.

Scene 7: Spot nice bracelet in jeweller's window. Would suit one of the young ladies in our family but we're not setting foot in the place on principle, as there are no prices displayed.

Scene 8: Enter fashionable deli, keen to support independent traders, but since neither of us has bought our specs, we can't tell what most of the stuff is. Leave with a portion of very smelly cheese and only realise later that it cost £25 per kilo – more than fillet steak. For 'fashionable' read 'rip-off'.

Scene 9: Another refuelling stop. Order a drink apiece and a gooey citrus tart. 'Would you like two forks with that?' asks charming young assistant, thinking, 'Tight old gits.'

Scene 10: Back home eight hours after we set out. Wife's rubbing at a painful spot on her brow. 'You know,' she says, 'I think I've been bitten by something.'

'Blimey,' I say, 'it must have been desperate.'

Give me my inner Gandhi

ALL I want for Christmas is… a frugal one.

Growing up in the 1950s and '60s, Christmas Day was a truly mouthwatering prospect. As in most working-class homes, there was never an abundance of rich food and, birthdays aside, it was the only day of the year that brought new toys.

A roast dinner with all the trimmings was an annual treat. We kids could even endure Christmas pudding, because it came with a slug of Dad's rum instead of brandy in the white sauce and our loving parents had hidden coins in the goo with never a thought that we might swallow them and end up in A&E.

For most of my adult life, however, I've been lucky enough to be in work and able to enjoy such meals not once a year but once a week. And, delicious as they are, they're no longer special. Christmas Day is like every other Sunday, but squared: a vast meal with several types of meat, washed down with wine, finished with mince pies soaked in cream and followed by hours of loafing, bloated, in front of rubbish TV, daring myself to scoff one more chocolate, until evening comes and it's time for cheese and biscuits, perhaps with a few lettuce leaves and tomatoes to counteract the day's excesses.

I've been saying for years that we should to do something different at Christmas, to make it a unique event in the calendar. My wife agrees to the extent of having beef instead of turkey but can't get enthused about my more radical idea: a Christmas of anti-excess – no cards, because they're a waste of money; no gifts, because everyone we know has enough already; no rich food; and no use of gas or electricity.

I would discover my inner Ghandi, wearing only a loin cloth and sitting as cross-legged as a bad knee allowed while contemplating my good fortune as half the world struggled for survival.

'This is how I came into this life,' I would say to myself (because by now the missus would have hot-footed it to the relatives' for turkey and central heating), 'and this is how I will leave it.'

Such deprivation would give me a new sense of being, reawaken my wonder at the world around me and make me appreciate the gifts of warmth and nourishment as I stared at four walls in fading light, with only brown rice, water and uncooked vegetables for sustenance, in penance for decades of gluttony and extravagance.

I might learn a few Buddhist incantations in advance, to pass the time, but my day would otherwise be devoid of all forms of entertainment: no books, newspapers, TV, mobile phone or computer.

In this altered state, I might discover uncomfortable things about myself. Perhaps the true meaning of Christmas would become clear again as the Christian upbringing I abandoned long ago forced its way into my consciousness.

I might even come to consider myself not such a republican after all but one grateful to live under a monarchy, whereupon, squinting at the clock at the hour of the Queen's Speech, I might swap my loincloth for a pair of Union Jack boxers and run into the street, singing the national anthem.

And when at last sleep beckoned, I would shuffle off, smug and purified, to an empty bed, having first spelt out a message, in torn-up Brussels sprouts, inside the front door to greet my wife's return, 'Crack open the Quality Street, duck, and pop some cans in the fridge.'

Letter to Her Maj
To: The Queen, Buckingham Palace

Dear Your Majesty, I 'ope you'll forgive me for taking a liberty and writing to you at this busy time, when you've got all the presents for the royal 'ousehold to wrap (don't forget to use a cushion if you're doing it on your knees!) but I wondered if an 'umble servant might be permitted to make a suggestion.

It's about your speech, the one you'll be making on Christmas Day, when we all get round the telly before the Quality Street come out.

I don't know 'ow much you follow the news, Ma'am (I get most of mine off Facebook, but I never see you on there),` but there's something worrying us ordinary folk. It's about the kiddies – millions on 'em – goin' 'ungry.

It's not poverty like in our day – well, perhaps not yours, Ma'am – when we was lucky to 'ave a slice of bread and dripping, and some torn-up newspaper in the outside lavvie. But you're classed as poor now if you're on less than 17 grand a year, and that's nowt for a family, is it? Not enough to keep the little uns warm and fed and clothed like they should be under a modern monarch like your good self.

What makes it worse is all the rich so-and-so's, if you'll pardon my French. Did you know there's over two million millionaires in this country? That 'oover man, Sir James Dyson, he's top. Worth £16 billion, they reckon. And there's at least 50 more of 'em, BILLIONAIRES, living under Your Majesty.

I were in the dentist's the other day and were looking at one of them posh magazines and it were full of Christmas gift ideas and there were a man's watch for SEVENTY THOUSAND POUNDS! It just don't seem right, Ma'am, 'specially when them at the bottom have 'ad it 'arder then most with the coronavirus an' all, what with short time and losing their jobs, then struggling to pay the rent. They're gonna suffer next year, jabs or no jabs.

Anyway, I've troubled you long enough, Your Majesty, so I'll get to the point. I were wondering, if you hadn't quite finished writing your speech, if you could make a little appeal to all the rich folk to chuck a thousand quid each in a pot to 'elp the poor?

Them tycoons wouldn't miss it at all but just think what two million thousand quids could do for the 'ungry kiddies!

I'm sure they'd all agree if it came from you, Ma'am. In fact, I reckon they'd be embarrassed to turn you down.

And I think I can speak for most of your 'umble servants when I say we wouldn't mind if you kicked things off with a grand from the royal coffers what we give you.

BEING GRANDAD

Babysitting the grandparents, by Harry Pheasant, aged six weeks

WELL, this is it: my first babysitting shift with the grandparents.

It's me doing the looking-after, of course. Mummy and Daddy are leaving me for the first time since that messy business four weeks ago, the day I came out. I'd got so comfortable in there. 'You'll be a good boy for Mamma and Grandad, won't you?' they say. Other way around, methinks. Like that, 'methinks'? See, I was concentrating in Womb School; took it all in from the voices outside. Know loads of words, I do. Just need time to make the noises *they* can understand.

Mamma and Grandad: now, she's the batty one with the big smile. Keeps making funny faces at me – all wide eyes, and popping sounds with her lips. I guess she means well.

And he's the one with the shiny head. Got less hair than me.

That's them arriving. 'Aw, he's asleep, bless him.' That's Mamma.

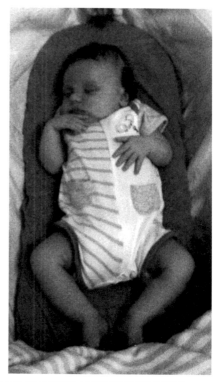

Yes, I'm asleep but I can still hear you. And what are you doing? What's that you're putting over me? A blanket? I was quite warm enough, thank you very much, but now you'll have to cuddle me – and you've only just got here. This won't look good on your report.

'His ickle eyes are open, Pete. Shall we get him out?'

Course you shall! But just watch the neck. I'm still working on the floppy head thing.

Mmm, nice rocking action, Mamma. And here come the kisses. Yes, I know I'm

Just because I'm asleep doesn't mean I can't hear you.

gorgeous. And I've got a cute ickle nose. And you could eat me all up. And… steady on! Doesn't the old man feed you?

Waaaaaaaa!

That's 'give me milk' to you. Now hurry up and get it mixed and… nm nm nm nm.

Waaaaaaaa! Who said you could stop? Yes, I have got a bottom lip, haven't I? And what's with the back-patting? That's not a windy look I'm wearing, that's a smi…

Urrrrp!

'Good boy!'

OMG. Anyone'd think I'd done something clever. Now feed me!

'Does he want more bock-bock, does he?'

No, he wants his bottle! Why don't these people talk properly? Pop it back in. Nm nm nm nm zzzzzz.

Right, you've had 15 minutes' rest. Can't you see my leg sticking up?

'Come to Grandad, little Haribo.'

Do not EVER call me Haribo!

Yes, I'm wet. So get me on that mat and… ah, fresh air down below, sweeeet! And a big raspberry on the belly button. Oops, here comes the magic fountain.

'Aw, he's wee-weed all over Grandad's T-shirt. Good boy!'

See how easily amused they are at this age?

And what do you mean, 'he can't want more milk'? Nonsense! Tip it up, old man, all the way. Fill me with air and you'll regret it, I tell you. And don't whip it out until the moment I stop.

Now where's he putting me? Over the shoulder, eh? Well, here's a milky mouthful down his back for his troubles. Now he's got my head in his hot armpit and he's swinging this way and that and singing something about forever blowing bubble… zzzzzz

'Has he gone to sleep, Pete?'

'Think so. Back to bed he goes. Bet he's awake again in ten minutes, though.'

LOL. You won't get that long, sunshine. See that ickle hand I'm sticking up? And see that ickle finger? Well, that's what I've wrapped you around tonight. And I've only just begun.

A world of wonder

ENCHANTED, bewitched, infatuated, smitten, enraptured…there's not a word in the dictionary to adequately describe what it's like to be a grandad.

Six months into the role, I'm utterly besotted with our little Harry.

It's not merely the boy himself; not just the slightly chubby legs that pump with – what: excitement? anticipation? curiosity? – when he sees my face on those visits that can't come soon enough; not only the smiles that, with growing regularity, crease a face that remind me sometimes of his mum, sometimes of his dad but always of a unique mini-man fast developing a look and personality all of his own.

It's not simply the eyes brimming with inquisitiveness as I hold him in strained arms and show him the wonders of the world: the large clock on our living room wall, the contents of the fridge, the stripes of our wallpaper – anything; nor the two front teeth he likes to test on my finger before feeling in my mouth for something similar; nor the song-like murmurings from his cot that wake us hours before we're due when he stays over at ours and sleeps so long and silent that we can't settle in case he's stopped breathing.

It's not just the smell of his head or the oh-so-kissable neck or the way his brow furrows, his cheeks redden and his arms and legs stiffen at meal times as he shouts 'erh!' because the spoonful of carroty mush that Grandad's turned into an aeroplane is taking way too long to land.

All of this is magical enough but the joy of grandparenting is also about something I hadn't given much thought to before Harry's arrival: the delight of watching your own offspring enjoy what you went through with them. Pleasure by proxy.

There are so many things you can explain to your own children but no amount of detail does justice to the role of being a parent.

Let's face it, when your first child arrives, you have no idea what you've let yourself in for. But when they have a child of their own, you know exactly what's coming. So, not only do you have the best seat in the house at a show starring the funniest creatures in creation (without the toil of nurturing and keeping them safe every day) you can appreciate the life-changing, fun-filled – and sometimes scary – journey your own offspring is experiencing.

I'm writing this on Mother's Day and, though my own dear mum is long gone, I can share my daughter-in-law's delight on discovering that, after she and Harry have dozed off on the sofa together, she'll awake to find him smirking into her face. And I know that the smiles that greet my son on his return from work will be enough to banish all the blues of the day.

Children aren't for everyone, of course. Many couples are gloriously happy without them; others, sadly, don't have the choice. To those who do and are thinking of starting a family, I say: don't make your parents wait too long for the best gift of all.

The grandparent elixir

DO you ever find yourself wondering: where has all the energy gone?

Do you hanker after some dim and distant time when you'd wake up feeling fresh and full of vim? Remember that feeling of 'oomph', a burst of life that thrust you up through the gears like a boy racer with a NOx exhaust?

And now? You've spent so long chugging along in fourth at 29mph that you begin to wonder if those explosions ever happened.

You are not alone. I am privileged, however, to have access to a magic potion second-hand. I find it in Grandad Land.

From the moment he stirs at six in the morning my potion peddler, 18-month-old Harry, is on the go.

He'll talk to his teddies in a stream of babble rich in intonation before crying for our attention, then wriggle into our bed, shouting, pointing, laughing, raspberry blowing; fingers picking at eyebrows and ears (ours); arms and legs pounding delicate bodily parts (ours).

He'll scramble on to the floor to find his pre-breakfast bottle, wave it demandingly in our direction and lie back to enjoy it – but with deceitfully sleepy eyes, for as we embark on a futile attempt to 'have another hour's kip', he'll half cuddle one, then the other and swing his little head around like a demolition ball until 'Ma-ma' gives in and takes him downstairs while 'Gyanda' has a lie-in, male chauvinist pig that he is.

The bomb site that greets me eventually is a sign that he's in full throttle. He's already devoured one and a half breakfasts and, after sampling mine, is ready to run me ragged for the next four hours. With my utter compliance.

One minute we're feeding torn-up tissue paper to his plastic zoo animals, the next we're kneeling on a hard floor as he arranges magnetic figures on the fridge door and smiles when I congratulate him on identifying a six – though he insists on calling every figure 'seex'.

Or we're filling his toy car with petrol or scribbling furiously with crayons, or piggybacking, or bouncing balls. And chasing, always chasing: him running like a duck, me with aged back bent and arms outstretched in fear of a tumble (by me). And umpteen games of peep-bo in which Harry the hider can clearly be seen, but that doesn't matter as long as he can't see us.

I used to be sniffy about people who left the TV on all day but I have to admit that background CBeebies is a godsend. A few minutes in front of *Twirlywoos*, sharing a biscuit with Harry and his soft-toy pal Tigger, allows me to catch my breath – and Harry to fully recharge his battery.

He's soon leading Gyanda and Ma-ma into the front room to observe the ritual of ring-a-ring-o'-roses at precisely the same spot where we played it a week ago.

High on giggles and lack of oxygen, one of us mentions a leg-and-a-wing and he instantly flops to the floor, ready to be swung and tossed in a beach towel and to greet every 'very big three!' with a little finger crooked in front of his face that says 'just one more'.

It's not yet midday and there's still time to be led upstairs to dance around his cot to Bob Marley and play splish-splash in the bathroom before lunchtime brings an excuse to imprison the whirling dervish in his highchair for half an hour.

I ache all over as I head for work. But a few drops of the elixir are coursing through my veins and I know I can look forward to a normal night of fitful, toilet-disturbed slumber later. Harry, meanwhile, will be deep in dreamland for 11 hours with barely an interruption.

Remember sleep like that?

New kid in town

ALLOW me to introduce myself. My name is Jasper Thomas Pheasant and I'm one year, four months and three days old.

I thought it was about time I made a few things clear. I've spent all my life so far in the shadow of the exalted one, my big brother King Harry. This has certain advantages because while he's being shouted at, I can do what I please. I mean, no one's going to shout at a baby, right?

But it seems that I'm 'at that age' when I have to be 'given certain rules'. I've heard Mummy say I'm getting to be to be a right little terror. Daddy even put me on the Naughty Step the other week and all I'd done was bite Harry's tummy because he'd pushed me over.

Me having a posh meal.

So, I thought I should lay down a few rules of my own to help the oldies understand how things are going to be around here:

- Do not disturb me when I'm in Poo Corner, which is wherever I choose it to be.
- The contents of cupboards, drawers, bowls, purses and other receptacles shall be sought out and emptied on to the floor. It's the law.
- If it looks like a sweet, I'll eat it. Especially if it's a stone.
- There is no such thing as a single biscuit. Mamma says so.
- What's on my plate is mine, except when it's mushed up and offered to you in my fingers. What's on your plate is also mine.
- Viewing the contents of my nappy is not an excuse to hold your nose and shriek 'phew!' And yes, it gets everywhere, doesn't it? Working it into all those creases takes lots of practice, you know. Talking of stinkies, what DOES Grandad drink at bedtime? Cabbage water?

- I shall not be held responsible if blowing on, kissing or otherwise tickling the tummy area causes The Fountain to go off.

- Where Harry goes, I will follow. What he does, I will do. But don't be fooled: he might be bigger than me now but I'll always get the sympathy vote. And when he's an old man of 30, I'll still be in my 20s.

- Do not try to stop me playing with the TV remote control. I know what the volume button does and you WILL hear it DEAD LOUD.

- In hide and seek, I will always hide where I just found you hiding. By the way, Grandad's not allowed to play this game because he's started doing sorcery: the other day, I waved to him as he drove down the road and when I went upstairs, he wasn't in bed. He's ALWAYS in bed.

- Failure to observe any of the above may result in the appearance of my bottom lip, which I'm told makes me look sooooo cute. If this happens, I expect a cuddle within five quivers. Or else.

WORDS

Oiling the blather machine

CALL me paranoid if you will but I sense a plot by bureaucrats and PR persons to send the rest of us loopy.

I'm convinced they're trying to trick ordinary folk into thinking the world around them has changed beyond recognition, by introducing a whole new language.

I mean, what existed between buildings before we had open spaces?

How did communities manage before social cohesion?

Did things ever start before they were up and running?

Did people make time for appointments before they had windows, or work together before partnership approaches?

Were government departments useless before they weren't fit for purpose?

Were things OK before they were not a problem?

Before every new project became an initiative, did we show any?

Did firms cut jobs before they downsized?

I'm sure I saw bobbies on the beat before we had high-visibility police patrols.

But I wonder if shops knew how many customers they'd had before footfall was invented.

It's not that I'm against everyday language evolving. It's just that I hate new words and phrases that fog the issue or make it harder to understand what used to be easy. And there's a whole highly paid industry doing just that.

I used to think prison officers tried to get old lags back on the straight and narrow with a bit of education – until I read some government PR blurb about 'initiatives to reduce re-offending and prepare prisoners for a crime-free life on release, including education skills training regimes and substance abuse courses'.

Blather.

When a group of teenagers created posters to give a positive message about young people, a council spokesman declared that they'd 'played a role in informing the city's Children and Young People's Plan, which guides the policies and actions of all agencies working on behalf of children and their families'.

Piffle.

And when a charity organised a family picnic in a park, a hyphenated spokeswoman whinnied, 'It's so empowering for people to meet over a shared bond.'

For heaven's sake, they were having fun and ice cream!

I'd often wondered what a library was. Then I came across a newspaper report about one being built near my home, with a councillor saying it would be 'a hub for community learning and information and a catalyst for community empowerment'.

Funny, that's just what they were saying down at the King's Head.

Good news is good news, though, no matter how it's dressed up and so I was pleased to learn that a law firm was in need of more staff, or as a spokesman put it, 'We're anticipating further recruitment during the year as we seek to resource what is a well-populated forward transaction pipeline.'

I'm off to find a bladed instrument with which to release a watery substance rich in cells and platelets from my lower arms.

Job titles lost in hot air

THIS won't enhance my credentials as a grumpy old windbag but I have a confession: I'm not in the habit of criticising local councillors.

I don't share the view that they're only it for what they can get. I've met hundreds over the years and most have struck me as being motivated by a desire to help others. Initially at least.

They might make a few grand in allowances for going to meetings but it's peanuts beside the sums paid to council staff – those who wield the real power in local government and can't be kicked out at election time.

You might have guessed there's one coming, so here's the 'but': I'm sick of the pompous titles some of today's senior councillors bestow upon themselves.

Once upon a time those who did well became chairman of committees – housing, recreation, health, finance; things we could understand.

Now, they're getting too big for their boots. Consider the following incredible but true titles, gleaned from local newspapers:

Portfolio holder for area working, cleansing and community safety. What, for heaven's sake, is 'area working'? I wonder if this role extends to cleansing souls, or even soles.

Cabinet member for safe and strong. Strong what? Toilet paper?

Cabinet member for clean and green. As opposed to dirty and brown, I presume.

Head of community shaping. He or she is no doubt in charge of creating upright citizens and rounded individuals.

The police are no better. Instead of town centre cop shops, which actually made people feel safer, we have 'safer neighbourhood teams' in case we don't understand the primary role of a police offer. Some of these wear 'high-visibility' patrols, as opposed to those we can't see.

But academia rules in the world of daft titles. Kids no longer go to school after the age of 11. They attend 'academies' or 'colleges' or even 'specialist colleges'.

A college is, by definition, an institution of higher learning, so what's higher about the local comp?

There are still primary schools, of course (renamed learning centres in some areas) and nurseries have yet to be renamed 'no-pressure introductory learning facilities in a socially inclusive environment' – but give them time.

And if secondary schools are colleges, where do kids – I mean young adult service users – go afterwards? Big College? Baby University?

Luckily, there's still a way to tell a proper college from a school: proper colleges boast the ponciest job titles. One really does have a 'vice-principal for learner voice, services and reputation'.

There's also a university with a 'director of lifestyle'. I'd love to know how that goes down with a bunch of bright, young, hedonistic freshers who left home precisely to escape older people telling them how to live.

There's no finer antidote to language-mangling than a bit of plain speaking and while scanning the dating pages of a regional newspaper (purely in the interests of research, you understand) I came across this appeal by a lovelorn gent who'd clearly decided that honesty was the best policy, 'Fifty-three-year-old male, short, fat, ugly, skint, looking for a lady with a good sense of humour.'

I do hope it worked.

Yufe-speak for grown-ups

YOU might have noticed a news item about the secret language used by teenagers online. Police in Nottinghamshire published a list of the terms, hashtags and acronyms that young people use to keep nosey parents in the dark.

The idea is to alert adults to what's really being said online in the hope that they will be better equipped to keep their children safe, from each other and from paedophiles out to groom them.

Among the 'warning flags' deciphered are #deb for depression; 420 (marijuana); CD9 (parents are around); ASL (age, sex, location); IWSN (I want sex now); merked – really drunk/beaten up/found out/told off); Molly (the drug ecstasy); sket (insulting term used towards girls); wavey (drunk or high); and zerg (to gang up on someone).

'Terms to keep an eye on' include 'Are you parring me?' (are you showing me disrespect?); begfriend (someone who sucks up to someone else); butters (ugly person); IANAL (I am not a lawyer); NAGI (not a good idea); PAP (post a picture); QQ (crying); SWYP (so what's your problem?); and WTPA (where's the party at?).

If some of that sounds sinister, a list of 'fun terms' reminds us that they're still just kids – baffed, for instance, for confused; DWBH (don't worry be happy); GOAT (greatest of all time); obvi (obviously); straight fire (something hot or trendy); and 'you da real MVP' (thanks for doing a mundane but important job).

Far be it for me to belittle anything that helps to keep young people safe online but this is yet another example of how the kids are taking over; how a world that once made sense is becoming ever more bewildering to those of my generation. So, for the sake of balance, perhaps we should start our own code: a dictionary of secret terms for old fogeys, to keep young noses out of our business.

Here are a few to get your juices flowing:
- AJs – aching joints
- Bostin – in urgent need of a toilet
- Crikey – OMG
- 2.30 – dental appointment
- FJ2D – flu jab today
- Fun – funeral

- Gor blimey – he/she should could change my dressings any day
- LMG – lost my glasses
- MUFTAB –meet up for tea and biscuits
- PM in H – putting me in a home
- S&M – sausage and mash

Cops in his underpants

I'VE been looking through a little treasure chest and thought I'd share the contents.

It's a file I kept over many years as a newspaper subeditor and proofreader. 'Subs', as they're known in the trade, are the people tasked with designing pages, making reporters' stories fit the space allocated for them, making sure they're accurate, grammatical and follow the paper's style and spotting potential libels that could land their bosses in court.

Newspaper production is one mad rush and what might seem fine when written in the race to a deadline can be misinterpreted or look plain silly in cold print, with a wrong word chosen or a sentence poorly assembled.

Even with subeditors and page proofers in place, howlers slip through. One former colleague still shudders at the memory of his (published) headline about a 'pubic inquiry'.

Here are a few more I kept from a waiting world:

- Parish councillors are calling for pedestrian refugees to be installed in a busy road
- The principal guset at the club's dinner was…
- A student who died in a plane crash will be awarded her degree post humorously
- Mini-motorbike owners who cause a nuisance with the machines are being warned they could be seized and crushed
- My father-in-law used to drink there with his belated wife
- Game tackles prostrate cancer
- He has now completed a furher education course
- Medication has been stolen from a house that could be dangerous if consumed by the wrong person
- A week of community action involved councillors highlighting the problems of dog fouling. Sports clubs also opened their doors for free taster sessions
- The Lord Mayor said he was honoured to be asked to light the Market Square beacon with an Army Cadet

Police officers have been getting up to some odd things, according to these examples:

- The prosecutor said ******* had been spotted by a PCSO threatening another man with a baseball bat
- The man was charged after drugs were found by police hidden in his underpants

The unfashionable Oxford comma would avoid misunderstanding in this example:

- The website showcases the bizarre champions of the online universe, including a man who picks his nose with his own tongue and the world's greatest petrol pump attendant

And the often-ignored hyphen can make a world of difference:

- The Model Railway Club is welcoming miniature railway enthusiasts
- The green fingered couple are opening their garden to the public
- Heavy rock singer dies

But it's the smutty ones I like best. One of my editors was fond of saying that 'subs' should have the cleanest copy and the dirtiest minds. He'd have liked this headline:

- Couple meet on the job, then marry

And this, from a woman interviewed on the occasion of her 100th birthday:

- 'Religion has definitely helped me in life. I used to go to the church but now the vicar comes and gives me a service in my home.'

The wong words

I COULDN'T resist digging out a few old books after another example of political correctness made headline news.

Publisher Harper Collins announced that it was removing a character from the forthcoming update of David Walliams's book *The World's Worst Children*.

Out goes Brian Wong, Who Was Never, Ever Wrong, after a podcaster named Georgie Ma complained that the character was 'normalising stereotypes on minorities from a young age'.

Poor Brian is portrayed as a Chinese boy with glasses and small eyes. 'The overall character,' said Ms Ma, 'plays on the model minority myth where Chinese people are nerdy, swotty and good at maths, we're not confrontational and we're high achievers.'

I can think of worse stereotypes. The book's other characters, for instance, include a victim of head lice (Nigel Nit-Boy), a girl let down by her parents in the personal hygiene department (Grubby Gertrude) and a sensitive soul called Bertha the Blubberer.

But I'm from a different era and hate to think what Ms George would have made of some of the characters in my 1972 *Dandy* annual, featuring the likes of PC Big Ears, Corporal Clott, a teacher called Greedy Pigg and two Chinese spies named Wun Tun and Too Tun, who say things like 'velly good way of getting over big fence into secret Blitish Base'.

Language changes with time. Words and phrases that seem acceptable in one era are, naturally, deemed offensive in later, more enlightened times. Imagine the outrage if old shows like *Till Death Us Do Part* and *Love Thy Neighbour* appeared on primetime television today.

I have a cherished set of books called *Lands And Peoples*, published almost 100 years ago. They strike me as being very sensitive – of their time – in their vivid descriptions of a world that white British youngsters in the 1920s could only imagine, long before television in homes, yet they are littered with descriptions that would have been deemed offensive even in my school days. One picture caption refers to 'the Fuzzy Wuzzies of Abyssinia'; another declares, 'The negro's idea of music is a good loud noise.'

We move on, thank goodness.

Chinese spies Wun Tun and Too Tun from The Dandy annual in 1974.

But there are some daft and disturbing examples of the language police at work.

Author and former teacher Kate Clanchy has been forced to rewrite her award-winning memoir *Some Kids I Taught And What They Taught Me* because she referred to 'chocolate-coloured skin' and 'almond-shaped eyes'.

Objectors said such language was 'dehumanising' and commodifying'. As one put it, 'There are many plenty of ways to describe POC [people of colour] ... that don't need to be related to food. It's delicious but we're not edible. We're people!'

Good job my parents aren't around these days. They might find themselves in hot water for calling someone or other a 'silly sausage' or a 'good egg'.

HOLIDAYS

You can't beat the English seaside

I'VE been having great fun getting soaked and shivering in a state of near-nakedness.

I'm at a rather delicate age, a time when foolish, feeble men indulge themselves in the pursuit of lost youth, but allow me to put your mind at rest: I've not joined a fetish club or done anything likely to outrage public decency.

I've simply rediscovered the English seaside.

After several years of holidaying abroad, we took our sons, aged 16 and 19, for a week of self-catering in Devon.

They're old enough to go their own way, so if the prospect of a hillside ramble with the oldies didn't light their fire, they could always slob in front of the telly. Besides, we thought it might be our last family holiday before grandchildren arrived and a free babysitting service was required.

For once I vowed not to spend the entire holiday behind the wheel in search of favourite resorts.

But day one was still rubbing the sleep from its eyes when I piled us into the car and drove ten miles to the lovely beach at Woolacombe.

I needed to smell the sea. I needed sand between my toes. Above all, I needed to be tossed about in salt water.

The boys had always shared my love of the sea and, as long as the weather was warm enough to strip to shorts on the beach, we'd brave the waves.

Warm, clear Mediterranean waters have their own magic but there's one thing that sets the British seaside apart: no matter how warm the weather, the sea is always f-f-f-freezing.

No sooner had we set up camp on the soft sand than the three of us were charging towards the crashing foam.

The lads plunged straight in, while I observed one more ritual that has given them cause to poke fun at me: I was not going past my knees, I insisted. It was too cold. Just a paddle…

But the pull was irresistible and I quickly shuddered through the pain barriers – knees first, then naughty bits, then waist, then – God, it's cold! – nipples and, finally, all the way under, My head felt as if it had turned to ice. But in that moment, I remembered why I loved it so. It was pure, free, breathless, gloves-off excitement and I giggled like a lunatic as each wave made me gasp and tried to knock me off my fee.

All around me were more reserved souls, surfers of varying ages and agility, dressed in wetsuits to dull the sea's sting.

They can keep their protective layers. I wouldn't miss the sharp edge where pleasure meets pain for all the world.

As I raced the boys back to our outstretched towels, knowing that I'd soon be asleep in a strange bed, with my creases full of sand and my hair twisted and stiff from salt shampoo, I knew that my holiday had truly begun.

The horrors of shorts

DEPARTURE minus four days: me and the missus are going on holiday.

It's 21 years since we had more than a day on our own, ever since we traded in our brains for the parent model, and we're wondering how we'll cope.

Will we be fit to kill each other by the end of it? Or will it be a heavenly week of sand, sun, sea and… sleep?

Will she be driven into the arms of some slinky-hipped Spanish waiter as I fall prey to that holiday sickness that makes men's eyes linger on female forms other than their loved ones? It is a dreadful burden we chaps bear.

At least I've not had the hassle of deciding where to go this year. My wife booked us a late cheapie and the fact that I've had absolutely nothing to do with the arrangements will never be spoken of by me again. Honest.

We've had a week at home to avoid last-minute panics but three days have slipped by and we've still not been shopping, so off we set, armed with a list of holiday essentials, from flip-flops to insect repellent.

We're soon getting tetchy.

She buys a bikini and insists on keeping the hanger.

Me, 'Why do you need the hanger?'

She, 'Because they're useful. Anyway, you always forget them and we run out.'

Shop assistant, 'You tell him, love. Here, have a few more.'

She, 'Do you need deodorant?'

Me, 'No. Being smelly is one of the joys of being off work.'

She, 'I need some face cream.'

Me, 'That's true.'

I need some shorts but have never been a shorts person. Having what a friend's mum at primary school once called 'sparrow legs' (if only that woman knew what psychological damage she wrought!) I prefer the type that end halfway up the thigh because what bit of leg muscle I possess is there, but I'm told they're old-fashioned and fear I'd look like Charles Hawtrey from a *Carry On* film, prancing about a sea of well-honed bodies on the beach, yelling, 'Oh, I say!'

So, I head to the changing rooms with a few pairs of fashionably knee-length pairs, decorated like curtains from a 1970s B-movie, and settle on the least worst before discovering, to my horror, that they fasten at the front with two Velcro strips.

Is there no getting away from that wretched stuff? Can I really be confident that it will stay stuck in water?

I have visions of coming undone in front of a group of children and ending up in the Court in Brief section of the Menorcan Weekly Whatsit.

My legs look like turkey drumsticks. I'm convinced they wouldn't brown if I roasted them in 90-degree sunshine for a year.

And where did that roll of fat around my waist come from? These shorts are never size 34! Think I'll complain…

But as I reach the checkout – minus hanger – where the wife who'll tell me I look great in anything is patiently waiting to pay, I think: let's have the holiday first. Then she can strangle me.

Hotel Slobalot

ARE you in need of a break? Desperate to escape the lousy British weather? Just need to lie down somewhere warm and comfortable but can't afford to jet off to the sun?

Allow me to introduce you to Hotel Slobalot.

You needn't set foot out of the house and it won't cost a bean.

I've just checked in and feel like a celebrity. That's because I'm in my very own TV fantasy, loosely based on *The X Files*. The principal characters are Moulder and Scuzzy.

Last night's pots are swimming in cold, scummy water. I've been up for hours and haven't had a wash, let alone cleaned my teeth.

I'm wearing scruffy tracksuit bottoms and a tea-stained T-shirt. My feet are on the coffee table and I'm catching up on the weekend's newspapers while half watching *Bargain Hunt* followed by *Homes Under the Hammer* followed by *A Place in the Country*.

With luck, the day's biggest challenge will be to fend off a phone call from Mumbai asking if Mr Feezant realises that his computer is at risk or that he's eligible for a grant towards loft insulation.

I've breakfasted on a pile of Malted Milk biscuits and three cups of tea and can hear a chocolate éclair calling my name from the fridge.

It's heaven: a rare day with nothing to do but laze about. No showering, shaving and getting out of the house on time for work.

And, just once in a while, it's nice to have nothing to do and break all the rules.

Hotel Slobalot is the ultimate staycation; precisely not what the doctor ordered.

Exercise? I might go for a little walk to the shop three doors away to buy a newspaper. Or an ice-cream. Does surfing the internet count as exercise?

Five portions of fruit a veg? On any other day, perhaps. But today I'll mostly eat carbs, fat and sugar.

Come to think of it, I haven't had that prince among fast foods – cheese on toast – for ages. Now, where's that note I scribbled in the pub a few weeks ago, the one about different cheese on toast habits?

Ah! I find it in a jacket pocket and gradually discern the sort of momentous questions that beer teases from idle tongues. Brown bread or white? To toast one side or both before adding the cheese? Toast buttered or not? Cheese sliced or grated? With sauce or not? Which sauce? Red? Brown? Worcestershire? Does the sauce go under or over the cheese? And which cheese is best?

Life's full of difficult decisions.

But enough of this thinking malarkey. Today I've been smacked with the lazy stick, and when nature wields that awesome weapon, even the most resilient has to lie back and take it.

Right now, I don't have a rush in me. Think I'll pop an old *Match of the Day* on the telly and make another cup of tea.

Just got to get comfy on the sofa first. It's amazing how I struggle to sleep at night in a comfortable bed, yet when I lie down in the middle of the day in a lazy v-shape with my head on one arm of the sofa and my feet on the other, I can drop off in...

GETTING OLD

Chin food and odd socks

'OOH,' my wife said, pointing and laughing, 'you are getting old fast.'

Charming, I thought. Thanks very much

So that's what I get for a lifetime's devotion.

I know what she means, though.

There wasn't much cream on the pudding that rounded off our dinner earlier that day but I'd still managed to get a dribble from lip to chin.

Mind you, she's a fine one to talk. The night before, when we'd gone out for a few drinks, she'd ouch-ed and aargh-ed as she hobbled up the street like a deranged *Thunderbirds* puppet because of a recurring injury she calls 'a bone in me foot'.

Meanwhile, I was doing a passable imitation of a Maori dance while furtling with my undercarriage as a result of wearing a new pair of boxer shorts.

The joys of getting old, eh?

As a friend who's nearing 60 put it, 'You lose your hair but it sprouts from eyebrows, nose and ears, you can't go for a poo when you want one, you can't not go for a wee when you need one – and best of all, you know it's going to get worse.'

He's right about the hair. I pulled a corker from my ear last week and have become adept at removing nasal hairs with my finger ends (discreetly, of course, like when I'm stopped at traffic lights). And, rather worryingly, I quite like the pain.

Eyebrows are harder to maintain but our sons' girlfriends are beauticians, so they look after us in that department, though we're going to have to come up with an alternative long-term.

I've asked the missus to make a pact with me to protect us as we advance into old age. It would commit us to checking each other for sprouting hairs, chin food, soapy ears, shaving wounds, odd socks, skirt-in-knockers and other old fogey characteristics before we leave the house.

She said she'd think about it but I suspect she's forgotten. That's what we do these days.

Completely forgetting, in the blink of an eye, what it was you wanted to say or do is bad enough but it's the partial lapses that really betray the old prune in me, like the time I told a friend's daughter that I'd bought my trainers from that well-

known high street shop Shoe Locker, whereupon she shrieked with laughter and said, 'You mean Foot Locker, Pete!' and proceeded to tap me on the head with a loud 'bless!'

Or when I was stitched up by my elder son in a restaurant. Having forgotten my glasses (naturally) I couldn't read the drinks menu, so when I offered to go to the bar to get a round in, he told me to ask for a brand of Portuguese lager, the name of which, I later discovered, he'd deliberately mispronounced. That's why the barman gave me a funny look when I asked for three Super Cocks.

Injuries are another giveaway. Time was when a bump or a sprain would quickly pass but I've only just shaken off a bad elbow that had dogged me for months and now I have a grinding shoulder that gives an air of slapstick to certain basic toilet functions,

I realise that I have much to be thankful for: my health, a job I enjoy, food aplenty, a loving family, financial security – all of which probably puts me in a small minority worldwide. I've already exceeded the average life expectancy of almost the entire African continent.

I just wish that keeping the ravages of age at bay wasn't such hard work.

Tattooed wrinklies

IT'S rude to stare but I couldn't help it. The young woman who passed me in the street appeared to have a set of thick ear-to-chin sideburns. Then it dawned: they were part of the inky artwork that covered most of her face.

It's estimated that more than 12 million people in the UK have at least one tattoo. The art form has come a long way since a forearm anchor signalled a seadog, while nicotine-tanned scallies had 'love' and 'hate' on their knuckles. No body part is sacred, it seems.

And if there are some strange sights around now, imagine what nursing homes will look like in years to come, once the elaborate pictures that appeared sharp and vivid on young, healthy flesh have succumbed to the pallor and wrinkles of age.

Visiting an elderly relative in one of those institutions today might mean a whiskery kiss from a white-haired old dear with nothing closer to facial art than a dribble of tomato soup; the only pin about her person being the one fixing a cameo brooch to her crimplene dress.

Fast-forward 30 years and grannie's legs have shrunk. She once displayed a magnificent tiger tattoo across closed knees but it's turned into a cartoon cat with one nostril and two half-ears.

Her nose ring looks fine unless she's sneezed. She gave up on ear discs after one fell out at bingo but the lobe holes remain and when she sits outside, the wind whistling through them sparks panic among confused residents, convinced there's a fire alarm

In the communal garden sits an old geezer engulfed in vape smoke, his full-sleeve tats now resembling crocheted arm warmers. A second slouches in a zombie-like state, though no one's sure whether this is normal behaviour or the effects of mamba. A third feels a toilet trip coming on and wishes he'd never had that piercing 'down below' as a young stud.

I've yet to see evidence of lip discs being used locally but a forward-thinking government could help future generations by encouraging this ancient custom now.

Some tribes in Ethiopia are able, with careful planning, to accommodate lip discs 11cm in diameter.

That's large enough for a small meal. Just think how much nursing homes and hospitals could save on crockery and washing-up.

Grandma's teeth

MY grandma was 100 years old, with dementia setting in, when she had to endure a rare stay in hospital after a fall. She was clearly feeling confused when I paid her a visit.

She looked frailer than ever with her gums bared, so I steeled myself and asked if she'd like me to pop her false teeth in. I meant in *her* mouth, of course, but made a mental note to self just in case.

I don't know what it is about other people's teeth but I'm clearly not alone in finding them yukky, because when I asked a strapping male nurse if it was all right for me to do the honours, he asked if I'd like a pair of rubber gloves.

'I do all sorts for the old people on this ward,' he laughed, 'but I always wear gloves for teeth.'

So, I emptied the watery detritus from the little plastic tub in which Gran's gnashers had been kept overnight and set about inserting them.

I couldn't understand why the bottom set wouldn't go in. Surely, she hadn't shrunk that much in a few days?

I tried pulling her mouth wider and tilting the falsies this way and that but to no avail.

Eventually, she grabbed them and started to put them in the wrong way. I protested that she'd do herself a mischief but by now she was very irritated and finally shrieked, 'I should know what I'm doing with my bloody teeth!'

And then she turned the 'bottom' set around and slotted them comfortably where they belonged – on her top gums.

Put *Dad Dancing* on the telly

'COME on, stop being miserable. Let's have you on that dancefloor.'

Words that strike dread in the heart of the dad dancer.

There he is, savouring a pint while trying to talk over the disco to a distant relative of the happy couple at a wedding reception in a village hall or banqueting suite somewhere, anywhere – they all look the same – when someone decides he's not enjoying himself.

And so begins a tug of war that occasionally takes him into a throng of gyrating teenagers and aunts and grannies doing Skippy the Bush Kangaroo impressions around handbags, and there's no escape.

He jogs from leg to leg, pumps his arms like a choo-choo train, allows the head to loll from side to side and tries to throw in a pelvic thrust or winding waist, all the time thinking, 'Where's it all gone, the rhythm? What became of the Northern Soul star of my youth, with his splits, his claps and his spins?

'When did I turn into cardboard?'

Or he does what most dad dancers do: resist the tugging arm even if they have to grab on to a nearby table leg or curtain, and say, 'You must be joking. I need some more ale down me first.'

Yes, I know: it's sad when people can't 'enjoy themselves' without getting drunk. But don't you get it, ladies? We don't want to dance. Don't ask us to explain. We simply don't enjoy it any longer. OK?

No, we're not being miserable when we sit on our own in a corner of a noisy, flashing room while everyone else does the 'Birdie Song' or 'YMCA'. We might not be having the time of our lives but we're existing as sanely as we can, because we just want 'dos' like these to pass as quickly and painlessly as possible.

You go ahead and dance, girls. You love it and you're great at it. Enjoy. Just leave us in peace.

And then, finally, when we've had enough to drink, which means rather too much, then we dad dancers will strut our stuff, as long as they play 'Baggy Trousers' or 'Hi Ho Silver Lining' or anything else we can yell to as we wave our arms above spinning heads.

We'll last for ten minutes or so, then we'll be lathered in sweat and need a sit down and another pint.

But it's a spectacle not to be missed, a glimpse into the past, of times when dad was A Person in His Own Right and did the sort of things he warns his teenage sons and daughters against doing.

And all they can do is watch in toe-curling embarrassment as he flings his ageing frame around and makes unseemly waist movements, while older relatives and so-called pals cheer and capture the horrors on their mobile phones, to torment him in the months to come.

It took several decades of suffering before my idea dawned but now that it has, I can't believe no one else beat me to it and cashed in. I'm sure there's big money to be made.

Half the country is hooked on dancing, right? Just look at the success of TV shows like *Strictly Come Dancing*, *So You Think You Can Dance* and *Dancing on Wheels*.

I look forward to *Blind Tango Incontinent Elderly Dancing in Bed*.

So why not *Dad Dancing*?

It might take a big prize to lure contestants out of their shells but it would make great viewing.

This is how I see it working: each dad would be pitted against a teenage son or daughter. The first half of the show would be alcohol-free, with both showing off their moves to music chosen by the child. The second would follow a lengthy beer break, with music of the dad's choice.

Marks would be awarded for rhythm and agility on the one hand and pure cringeability on the other.

Remember: you heard it here first.

No escaping the bald truth

IT was a disturbing sight, the sort that, once glimpsed, can never be forgotten.

As the hairdresser finished his work and held a mirror to the back of my head, a hairless dome glistened beneath fluorescent lighting.

I'd turned into Friar Tuck's brother.

I knew it was coming. My sons had been teasing me about my 'bird's nest' for years. Now, the birds – herons, by the look of things – had evidently flown the nest and I was left with what my sister calls wavy hair: that is, it's waving goodbye to my head.

That I'd been rapidly losing my locks up front had been obvious for some time, even in my most deluded moments. But, perhaps in some innate sense of self-preservation, I've developed a habit of tilting my head forward when forced to look in a mirror these days and am forever surprised when the full extent of my hairlessness is revealed by my reflection in a shop window or computer screen.

Now I come to think of it, the hairdresser had never offered me a full-on top view before. He's a nice chap – and that's the point. We blokes have a shared philosophy when it comes to bodily matters: ignore it and it will go away. Besides, knowing it was there and seeing it in all its shiny glory are different things.

Now, I feel like I've looked Medusa in the eye and life will never be the same.

No longer can I ruffle the top of my head and think all's well. From this day forth, every drop of rain that falls will ping like a sledgehammer on my bald dome. It will be a target for popcorn flingers in cinemas, a landing strip for flies and something for kids behind me on buses to point and giggle at.

Perhaps I should swap my hairbrush for a tin of polish and a duster.

I might change my name to Pate Pheasant.

Alopecia is such a warm and cuddly word for such a bringer of doom. I bet it comes from the ancient Greek for 'revenge of womankind'.

At least it didn't afflict me in my 20s or 30s, or I might have joined the growing ranks of young men who shave their heads instead of letting nature take its course. Heaven knows I'm dangerous enough when I take a razor blade to my face, let alone something I can't see.

I just have to accept baldness as another sign or advancing years, like secondary eye bags, ear hair, and man boobs where once there was a hint of muscle.

And, looking on the bright side, what better characteristic could a professional grumpy old man hope for than a genuine, permanent monk-on?

All downhill from here

I'M sure you don't need me to tell you that time flies ever faster the older we get but have you noticed that there's a purple patch in this process, at around 55 to 65 years of age, when people suddenly look much older very quickly?

This struck me as I wandered around the shops in my home town and saw dozens of folk I'd either been acquainted with or recognised simply from living in the same community for many years.

We had all entered life's adult ranks at around the same time. Now, our active service days are numbered and we're heading for discharge, honourable or not.

Rapidly coming our way are the Four Ds: decay, decrepitude, dementia and death.

Never mind 'where did 40 years go?' what happened to the last five or ten? It seems I've barely blinked and the last vestiges of youth and rude health, still evident in our 40s and early 50s, have slipped away, leaving a whole generation grey/stooped/wrinkled/warty/bald/sagging/squinting/hard of hearing/shabbily dressed, or all of these, with bellies bulging in varying degrees and the spring in our step down to a few rusty, flattened coils.

We're all looking at each other and thinking 'hasn't he/she gone downhill?', which is why I spare myself a little misery by giving mirrors a wide berth, beyond checking for whatever my grandsons might have felt-tipped on my forehead.

But we're beautiful inside, eh?

And when infirmity finally takes away our independence, we might end up in a nice care home, like the one I visited on what would have been my father's 93rd birthday, to see his best mate, still a dear family friend 50 years after my dad's death.

They wheeled him out of a group session where a religious lady was leading a quiz about the Holy Spirit – see what fun you're missing, kids! – and we chatted in his room about times past and future prospects.

He had lost the use of one hand through a stroke but still clung to the hope that he would get well enough to go home. One day.

Rarely a week went by, he said, when he did not cry over the wife he had lost six years earlier, after six decades of marriage.

But there was a deep sense of satisfaction about him as he talked of his good fortune in living so long, having suffered his first heart attack at 42 and survived triple bypass surgery many years later; of the four children he and his wife raised and saw settled, with families and careers of their own; and of the joy of grandchildren, his pride evident as he spoke of one becoming a doctor.

His children visited regularly and were sorting out his financial affairs.

'They said I looked after them and now it was their turn to look after me,' he smiled.

Perhaps getting old isn't too bad after all.

THE END

The Whinger's days are numbered

REPORTS that the police want more Taser guns to help them combat violent criminals have alarmed civil liberties groups.

But a much bigger hoo-hah is about to erupt, because I can reveal plans to use a new electronic weapon to curb another type of social pest: the grumpy old man.

A secret Home Office study has concluded that firing 50,000 volts of electricity at bellyachers of a certain age who go around putting the world to rights would be excessive.

Instead, scientists have come up with a new stun gun. It's called the Daser and is set to silence elderly whingers.

While Taser gets its name from a fictional weapon – Thomas A. Swift's Electric Rifle – Daser stands for Disarm and Stabilise Elderly Ranters.

The device emits high-frequency waves, which are picked up by digital wristbands that all over-50s will be forced to wear on entering public buildings.

The result is said to be a numbing sensation that makes the silly old sausage forget what he – or she – was talking about just long enough to end confrontation, restore peace and send the whinger on their way home none the wiser.

'ERs (elderly ranters) are a well-meaning and generally law-abiding group,' says a leaked Home Office report

'They do, however, undermine government attempts to promote social cohesion.

'By venting their frustration and anger in public over minor failings by anyone from big businesses (eg, by telling supermarket checkout girls that they will report them to the company chairman for not saying "please") to private individuals (eg, chastising parents in the street for the behaviour of their children), ERs are widening the social divide.

'Such over-zealous self-righteousness carries two risks: 1, ERs may be subjected to physical abuse; and 2, more people may begin to behave like ERs but go on to make a fuss about bigger issues, such as the economy.

'Tests have shown that the Daser quickly and quietly immobilises ERs, with no lasting harm to the target.'

Unbelievable, isn't it?

I, too, was sceptical but am now utterly convinced, having put the device to the test.

I had to call in some big favours in Whitehall but finally tracked down the report's author and arranged for a demonstration. I'll call him D.

We met at my local swimming baths, where he handed me a wristband similar to those used for the lockers and told me to make a minor scene with another swimmer.

The prospect of such uncharacteristic behaviour made me slightly apprehensive but I swallowed my pride, attached the wristband, entered the water and launched into an old man's up-and-down swim routine. I could see D in the spectator gallery, holding what appeared to be a mobile phone.

Within minutes, I found my way blocked by two old biddies inching said by side in the water in a display of world championship nattering.

'Some people,' I muttered as we passed, 'have absolutely no manners.'

Suddenly, my wrist tingled. Then my body went numb and I was engulfed by a wave of pleasant memories. There was a song running through my head – 'Happy Daser here again' – and all I could think of was shop signs with apostrophes in the correct place and digestive biscuits dunked in strong tea.

I have no recollection of what happened from that moment until I arrived home half an hour later. However, D phoned to tell me I'd calmly climbed out of the water, waved goodbye to fellow swimmers, dressed swiftly and left the building with a broad smile.

Something tells me I should be disturbed by the Daser's implications for civil liberties. Truth is, I can't be bothered to complain.

BV - #0050 - 050522 - C0 - 234/156/8 - PB - 9781780916354 - Gloss Lamination